Maurice Baring
Letters

Maurice Baring

Maurice Baring
Letters

SELECTED AND EDITED BY

Jocelyn Hillgarth
& Julian Jeffs

MICHAEL RUSSELL

First published in Great Britain 2007
by Michael Russell (Publishing) Ltd
Wilby Hall, Wilby, Norwich NR16 2JP

Page makeup in Sabon by Waveney Typesetters
Wymondham, Norfolk
Printed and bound by Biddles Ltd
King's Lynn, Norfolk

Indexed by Jocelyn Hillgarth

ISBN 978-0-85955-309-4

Contents

Acknowledgements

Many have assisted us by providing letters or information about Maurice Baring and his circle, or both. We hope that those who are not mentioned by name will forgive us. Their contributions have been very much appreciated.

Louis Jebb, who has the advantage of descent from both the Baring and Belloc families, has provided a wealth of information and letters, many of which he has transcribed. He has made a major contribution. Other members of the family who have helped greatly include Maurice Baring's nieces Daphne Pollen and Victoria Ingrams. Another major contribution has been made by Mr and Mrs Ernest Mehew who assisted us with their deep knowledge of the life and literature of the period. The project began many years ago with a view to publication by the late Sir Rupert Hart-Davis but when he retired from his publishing house the project had to be abandoned; however he read through initial collections and made many helpful suggestions. Deborah Jeffs assisted with the chronology. Maurice Baring's executrix, the late Laura Lady Lovat gave the project her blessing, as did her daughter Veronica Lady Maclean and her son Sir Charles Maclean, Bt.

We would also like to thank all those who provided letters. Many of these are now alas dead. Where we know the present whereabouts of the letters we mention it. Our thanks are due to: the Berg Collection of New York Public Library for the letters to Sir Edward Marsh and E.V. Lucas; Merton College, Oxford for the letters to Sir Max Beerbohm; the Brotherton Library of the University of Leeds, the Bodleian Library of the University of Oxford and the British Library for the letters to Sir Edmund Gosse; the Jebb family for letters to Hilaire Belloc, now in Boston College; Mr Francis Warre Cornish for letters to members of the Cornish family; the University of Illinois for the letters to H.G. Wells; the Hon. Lady Salmond for the letters to Lady Desborough, now in the Hertfordshire Record Office; Mr Michael MacCarthy for letters to Sir Desmond MacCarthy and Raymond Abbott; Mrs Clare Sheppard for letters to Charlotte Warre Cornish; Miss V. A. Spencer Wilkinson for letters to Professor Henry Spencer Wilkinson, now with the Army Museums Ogilby Trust; Mr Raglan Squire for letters to Sir John Squire; the University of Texas for letters to Arnold Bennett; Leonard Woolf for letters to Virginia Woolf, now in the University of Sussex Library; Mr Alec Waugh for letters to himself, now at Sherborne School; Miss Evelyn Tatham for letters to her mother; the Strachey Trust for letters to Lytton Strachey, now in the British Library; Sir Michael Duff for letters to Lady Juliet Duff, now in the British Library. We apologise sincerely to any whose help has not been mentioned.

We must especially thank our publisher Michael Russell for his forbearance and for the immense amount of meticulous editorial work he put in, and Mr John Saumarez Smith for many helpful corrections, suggestions and additions. With so many letters to choose from we have no doubt that other editors would have chosen differently. We take full responsibility for having made the selection and for all mistakes.

Preface

Maurice Baring is not the force he was. The story is told of someone who went into a Charing Cross Road bookshop and asked 'Have you any Maurice Barings?' The reply was 'This is a bookshop, sir, not a garage.' He would have loved it. But in his lifetime he was a major literary figure: poet, novelist, humorist and Russian expert. His education had been in Latin and Greek but he was a remarkable linguist and had all the major European languages at his command, including Russian, and even a good knowledge of Chinese. He helped to introduce Russian literature into England by essays, translations and by editing *The Oxford Book of Russian Verse*. Both *Algae – an Anthology of Phrases* and his anthology (but it was much more than an anthology) *Have You Anything to Declare?* include selections from eight languages and in the latter there are many translations by himself. Although none of his books is currently in print, in his lifetime they were published in a uniform edition. He also had the distinction of being caricatured by Max Beerbohm and parodied in *A Christmas Garland* (second edition). When literary people are asked (usually around Christmas) for lists of forgotten books they still read and admire, his name is regularly mentioned, and his books are collected by a discerning group of followers. They have always been more popular in Catholic countries, notably France and Spain, where he is still highly rated.

His Catholicism was central to his life and to his novels, but although he is often associated with Belloc and Chesterton, his faith was very different from theirs. Belloc was born a Catholic. Baring and Chesterton were converts. Of his own conversion he wrote in *The Puppet Show of Memory*: 'On the eve of Candlemas 1909, I was received into the Catholic Church by Father Sebastian Bowden at the Brompton Oratory: the only action in my life which I am quite certain I have never regretted.' His Catholicism was of a more tolerant sort than Belloc's and he was not a theologian like Chesterton.

He first made his name as an authority on Russia. He travelled in

1904 to the Russo-Japanese war as correspondent for the *Morning Post*. There he attached himself to a fighting unit at the risk of his life. He repeatedly paid visits to Russia until the outbreak of the Great War. The Russian expert Sir Bernard Pares in his book *A Wandering Student* wrote that he was a

> ...former diplomat with the appropriate monocle, but with more acute understanding of Russian nature and character than any foreigner I have known and almost than any Russian. Baring's simple and clear vision had made the discovery that the greatest gentleman in Russia is the underdog soldier or peasant, and that was where he found his natural mates. 'Little Brother,' they would say to him, 'you are very bald', but they would speak out their hearts to him as perhaps to no one else. He discussed with them *Paradise Lost*, which was circulated in prose as peasant literature, or he would even tell them about Herbert Spencer. Baring's Russia is gone; but there is no book that will tell more of Russian character than his *What I Saw in Russia*, for he saw deep below the surface.

In 1907, when Russia was in chaos, Baring wrote that no one would know how it would end for another ten years. It was a sound prediction, the revolution coming in 1917. Another Russian scholar who had high regard for him was Isaiah Berlin.

Apart from his studies of Russia and its literature, he made his name as a humorist with three books: *Diminutive Dramas, Dead Letters* and *Lost Diaries*, later combined as *Unreliable History*. He was a very humorous man himself, full of tricks, jokes and whimsy. One of his most famous tricks was to balance things – usually a glass of wine or an egg – on his bald head. Before the First World War he had also published books of short stories and poems. Shortly after it he published *R.F.C. H.Q. 1914–1918*, based on his experiences as Lord Trenchard's ADC. In France he often put his life at risk, flying great distances and behind the lines in flimsy and unreliable aircraft. The book is an important historical source and was republished after the Second World War. He was a spectacular staff officer and Lord Trenchard's tribute to him is published as an appendix. Playing a considerable part in the foundation of the Royal Air Force, he was made an honorary wing commander.

The enormous range of his interests will be clear to anyone who reads these letters: his deep knowledge of literature in all the major European languages, his love of music, and not least his concern with the human situation not only in Britain but also in Russia, China and Ireland. He was a polymath with only one blank spot: mathematics.

His fiction came after the war. The short novels *Passing By* (1921) and *Overlooked* (1922) were apprentice pieces but show the formation of his unique style. Cyril Connolly wrote of it in *Enemies of Promise* (1938): 'There are, we know, many styles of vernacular: the colloquial language of Hemingway is different from the colloquial language of Maurice Baring yet each believes in informality and simplicity...' Although he made a reputation as a humorist, his novels make no attempt to be humorous and contain positively no purple passages, though many of the characters are clearly the creations of an author with a deep sense of humour. His austere style is now much more appreciated in France and Spain than in England, but it carries the story resolutely along, giving reality and insight to all the characters. Aside from his special importance to Russian scholars, *C* and *Daphne Adeane*, of his novels, and his wonderful autobiography *The Puppet Show of Memory* should assure him a place in literary posterity.

His letters were obviously appreciated by those he wrote to, as a great many have survived – of which this book contains less than a quarter. Apart from the difficulty of selection, there has also been the problem of transcription. Baring's handwriting was illegible and when he used a typewriter he hit the keys in such a haphazard way that the result was often little better. We have had to guess and no doubt others would sometimes have guessed differently, but we have preferred to do that rather than to pepper the text with question marks in brackets. Occasionally we have just left a bit out and marked the spot with dots.

A Brief Chronology

1874   On 27 April born at 37 Charles Street, Mayfair, the fourth surviving son of Edward (Ned) Baring, created Baron Revelstoke 1885, and his wife Emily *née* Bulteel.

1884   Went to St George's School, Ascot. He transferred with his younger brother Hugo to St Vincent's, Eastbourne.

1887   Went to Eton, Mr Heygate's House.

1888   Won the Trials Prize and the Brinkman Divinity Prize.

1890   In November the Baring bank faced a serious cash crisis and was rescued by the Bank of England with a consortium of banking houses. The family business was successfully reconstituted as a limited company – and the creditors paid off – by Maurice Baring's elder brothers John and Cecil, later respectively 2nd and 3rd Lord Revelstoke.

1891   Won the Prince Consort's French Prize.

1892   Left Eton and went to Hildesheim to learn German with a view to a diplomatic career. His mother died. The family's art collections were auctioned at a series of sales in London.

1893   Visited Heidelberg, Berlin and went to Bayreuth for the first time. In July met Edmund Gosse.

1894   Visited Florence. In August was sent to Mr Tatham in Abingdon to be coached for Cambridge. Went up to Trinity College in October.

1895   Left Cambridge at the end of the summer term having failed the mathematics paper in Little Go. Went to Versailles for a month and then back to Hildesheim. In September returned to London to be coached at Scoones for the Diplomatic examination which he failed to take owing to illness. Spent Christmas at Hildesheim.

1896   Failed the Diplomatic examination, again owing to mathematics. Visited Paris, Monte Carlo and Florence. Returned to Scoones for the summer term. In November took the Diplomatic examination and again failed.

1897   At the suggestion of Auberon Herbert went to Oxford to be coached but was never a member of the university. He had many friends in Balliol College, meeting Hilaire Belloc and Donald Tovey. Returned to Hildesheim in the Easter vacation. His father died, aged sixty-nine, in July. He moved out of the family house at 37 Charles Street and went to a crammer in Bournemouth.

1898   Passed the Diplomatic examination, having been given half marks in mathematics on account of his outstanding French. Entered the African Department of the Foreign Office.

1899   Appointed attaché in Paris. *Hildesheim: Quatre Pastiches* published.

1900   In August was transferred to Copenhagen, where he met the Count and Countess Benckendorff. Failed examination in International Law.

1901   On leave, he went to stay with Sarah Bernhardt at her home Belle Isle off the coast of Brittany. He also went to Russia to stay with the Benckendorffs and on his return to Copenhagen started to learn Russian.

1902   In January he transferred to Rome. In May he took a holiday on Mme de Béarn's yacht. In July he visited the Benckendorffs in Russia.

1903   Returned to London but visited Russia. *The Black Prince and Other Poems* and *Gaston de Foix and Other Plays* published.

1904   On 8 February the Japanese attacked the Russian Fleet at Port Arthur and torpedoed a ship – the *Revitizan* – on which Pierre Benckendorff was serving. M.B. returned to Russia on leave, installed himself with a Russian family in Moscow and worked hard at Russian. In April became war correspondent for the *Morning Post* and in June left for the Russo-Japanese war. He then returned to London and resigned from the Foreign Office.

1905   Wrote dramatic criticism for the *Morning Post* before returning to Russia. On 23 July the Duma was dissolved and there was a revolution. On 8 August left St Petersburg for Manchuria and remained until peace was declared on 1 September. Returned to London but was sent back to Moscow in October. *Mahasena* and *With the Russians in Manchuria* published.

1906   St Petersburg correspondent of the *Morning Post. Thoughts on Art and Life of Leonardo da Vinci* (translation), *Sonnets and Short Poems* and *Desiderio* published. His sister Margaret, Viscountess Althorp, died following the birth of her fifth child.

1907   From May to July returned to London and returned finally in December to live at 6 Lord North Street Westminster (since demolished). He was still in the employment of the *Morning Post. A Year in Russia* published.

1908   Held a great house warming party in Lord North Street. In the early summer his friend Henry Brewster died. *Proserpine* and *Russian Essays and Stories* published.

1909   In February received into the Roman Catholic Church. In April sent to Constantinople by the *Morning Post* and remained until the end of June. The *Morning Post* began to publish his series of 'Dead Letters'. *The Story of Forget-Me-Not and Lily of the Valley* and *Orpheus in Mayfair* published.

1910   *Dead Letters, The Glass Mender and Other Stories* and *Landmarks in Russian Literature* published.

1911   Moved to 33 Grosvenor Road, Pimlico. His play *The Green Elephant* was staged. *Diminutive Dramas, The Green Elephant, The Collected Poems, The Russian People* and *The Grey Stocking* published.

1912   In January sent to Russia to help with a visit of MPs, the Army, the Navy and the Church to the Russian Duma. Whilst in Russia conducted his only business ever for Baring's Bank. Set out for a journey round the world (later forming the book *Round the World in Any Number of Days*) which included a visit to New Zealand. In October *The Times* sent him out as war correspondent to the Balkans. His letters were later to be reprinted as *Letters from the Near East*. In December worked at the San Stefano Cholera Group. Moved to 32 Old Queen Street in Westminster which he shared with Auberon Herbert (Lord Lucas) and Auberon's sister Nan. On his return he was seriously ill and required an operation for an abscess. *The Double Game* published.

1913   The operation was performed in January and he went to Seville and saw a *corrida* in which Juan Belmonte performed. Returned to London at the end of April and went on a cruise in HMS *St Vincent* in June. In August went to Russia. *Letters from the Near East 1909 and 1912, Lost Diaries, What I Saw in Russia* and *Palamon and Arcite* published.

1914   Spent Easter at Seville and returned to England by sea. Visited Russia and then Constantinople where he stayed with the ambassador, Sir Louis Mallet. On the outbreak of war he joined the Army – with some difficulty owing to his age. Went to France with Sir David Henderson as a lieutenant in the Intelligence Department attached to the Royal Flying Corps, where he served for the rest of the war, becoming ADC to General Trenchard and rising to the rank of major. *Round the World in Any Number of Days, The Mainsprings of Russia* and *An Outline of Russian Literature* published.

1916   Prepared and published an anthology, *English Landscape*, in aid of the British Fund for the relief of Russian prisoners of war in Germany. *Translations (Found in a Commonplace Book)* and *In Memoriam Auberon Herbert, Captain Lord Lucas, Royal Flying Corps, Killed November 3, 1916* published.

1917   Appointed O.B.E. and mentioned in dispatches.

1918   Demobilised and was seriously ill. *Translations: Ancient and Modern* published.

1919   Moved into Pickwick's Villa, Dulwich. *Poems 1914–1917* published.

1920   *Poems 1914–1919, Manfroy* and *R.F.C. H.Q.* published.

1921   Went for a cure to Contrexéville. *Passing By* published.

1922   *The Puppet Show of Memory* and *Overlooked* published.

1923   Moved to 3 Gray's Inn Square. *His Majesty's Embassy and Other Plays* and *A Triangle* published.

1924   In January went on a Mediterranean cruise in HMS *Queen Elizabeth*, travelling home by way of Seville and Madrid. *C, Punch and Judy and Other Essays* and *The Oxford Book of Russian Verse* published.

1925   Spent spring with Admiral Fisher in Malta. Made honorary wing commander. *Half a Minute's Silence and Other Stories, Collected Poems, Translations Ancient and Modern (with originals), Cat's Cradle* published.

1926   Became ADC to Lord Trenchard during the General Strike, 3 to 13 May. His play *June and After*, translated as *Ihr Mutter Kind*, produced at the Berg Theatre, Vienna. It was his greatest critical success as a playwright. *Daphne Adeane* and *Last Days of Tsarskoe Selo* (a translation) published.

1927   *Tinker's Leave*, *What I Saw in Russia* and *French Literature* published.

1928   In January went to Gibraltar in HMS *Nelson* and then on to Malta in HMS *Resolution*, and was there when his nephew Cecil Spencer was killed in a riding accident. *Comfortless Memory* and *Algae* published.

1929   His brother John Revelstoke died in April, leaving him a legacy that eased his financial worries. *Fantasio* (a translation) and *The Coat Without Seam* published.

1930   Bought Halfway House, Rottingdean and was let a house at 18 Cheyne Row for a peppercorn rent by his brother Cecil. *Robert Peckham* published.

1931   Went on further cruises with the Navy. *In My End Is My Beginning* published.

1932   *Friday's Business* and *Lost Lectures* published.

1933   From January to March on a cruise in HMS *Hood*. In April mortgaged his house in Rottingdean to pay off most of his overdraft and moved out of Cheyne Row, selling some possessions and giving others to friends. He gave his collection of watercolours by Carmontelle, including the celebrated *Mozart Family*, to the Musée Carnavalet in Paris. *Sarah Bernhardt* published.

1934   In January went on a cruise in HMS *Hood*. *The Lonely Lady of Dulwich* published.

1935   In March and April took his last cruise with Admiral Fisher. From then the shaking that had affected him for many years was causing great difficulty and was diagnosed as *paralysis agitans* (Parkinson's Disease). *Unreliable History* and *Darby and Joan* published. Officer of the Légion d'Honneur.

1936   Too paralysed to write or travel. *Have You Anything to Declare?* published.

1940   His friend Laura, Lady Lovat, had him taken by train from Rottingdean to her house at Eilean Aigas, Inverness, to be away from the bombing of the South Coast.

1942 In February his house at Rottingdean was bombed, though not demolished. *Russian Lyrics* published.

1945 On 14 December died in Scotland, looked after by Laura, Lady Lovat.

Recipients

Balfour, Reginald (1875–1907). Educationalist and writer. Married Charlotte ('Scarlet') Warre Cornish. He met M.B at Cambridge, where he was later to become a fellow of King's College. His family had Russian commercial interests. His conversion to Roman Catholicism influenced M.B. He took his own life. Their daughter was Clare Sheppard (see Bibliography).

Beerbohm, Max (1872–1956). Caricaturist and writer. Educated at Charterhouse and Merton College, Oxford. Half-brother of the actor-manager Sir Herbert Beerbohm Tree. M.B. was the subject of two of his caricatures and one of his parodies. Knighted 1939.

Belloc, (Joseph) Hilaire (Peter) (1870–1953). Poet, historian, essayist, novelist and champion of Catholicism. Born in France of a French father and English mother. Educated at the Oratory School and Balliol College, Oxford where he was Brackenbury History Scholar and took a first in history. He met M.B. at Oxford in 1907. Became a naturalized British subject in 1902 and was a Liberal M.P. (1906–10). They are portrayed together with G.K. Chesterton in Sir James Gunn's *Conversation Piece*, described by one with as 'Baring, Overbearing and Beyond Bearing [Belloc]'. Knight Commander with Star, Order of St Gregory the Great, 1934.

Benckendorff, Countess Sophie (1857–1928). *Née* Schouvaloff. m. 1879 Alexandre, Count Benckendorff (1849–1917), diplomat; Russian Ambassador to the Court of St James (1903–17). M.B. met the Benckendorffs while en poste in Copenhagen in 1901. Sophie Benckendorff became M.B.'s principal muse and illustrated his children's book *Forget Me Not and the Lily of the Valley* (1909). Through this friendship M.B. became a Russophile and foreign correspondent in St Petersburg. Between 1906 and 1914 he spent much of each year at Sosnofka, the Benckendorffs' house near Kharkov. M.B. wrote a memorial poem to the Benckendorffs' son Pierre who was killed at the Battle of Tannenberg. After the war Countess Benckendorff's house in Suffolk became the repository of much Baring memorabilia.

Bennett, Enoch Arnold (1867–1931). Novelist, playwright and journalist.

Brewster, Henry (1850–1908). Author. Described by M.B. in *The Puppet Show of Memory* as '...an American by birth, a Frenchman by education, an Italian by residence'. A close friend of Ethel Smyth. He wrote the libretto for her opera *The Wreckers*.

Chesterton, Gilbert Keith (1874–1936). Novelist, critic, journalist and artist. He was part of a triumvirate with Baring and Belloc, and their triple portrait has been mentioned above. As an artist he illustrated some of Belloc's books. He met M.B. in about 1900 and had become close friends by 1922 when Chesterton became a Catholic. He wrote extensively on religious subjects. Baring pastiched Chesterton in *Round the World in Any Number of Days* (1919). Horne Fisher in Chesterton's book of stories *The Man Who Knew Too Much* is supposed to be based on M.B. One of the most popular authors of his day, now principally remembered for his Father Brown stories.

Cornish, Blanche (1867–1937), *nee* Ritchie. Biographer, was wife of Francis Warre Cornish and mother of M.B.'s friends Gerald, Hubert, Charlotte, Mary and Cecilia.

Cornish, Cecilia Warre. Daughter of Francis and Blanche Warre Cornish. She later married William Wordsworth Fisher, later Admiral Sir William, a frequent host to M.B. on Mediterranean cruises.

Cornish, Francis Warre, Vice-Provost of Eton and a celebrated figure at the school. The Cornish house, 6 The Cloisters, became a byword in the Baring family language for something familiar and reassuring.

Cornish, Hubert Warre (1872–1934), son of Francis Warre Cornish, a housemaster and later Vice-Provost of Eton. A scholar at Eton, where he was a contemporary of M.B., he went on to Cambridge as a scholar of King's. He became Senior Assistant Secretary of the Scottish Education Department. C.B.E., 1934.

Desborough, Lady, Ethel (known as 'Etty'), daughter of Hon. Julian and Lady Adine Fane; m. 1887 William Henry Grenfell, athlete, politician and banker, cr. Baron Desborough 1905. She led the clever upper-class coterie known as The Souls and was known for the charm of her Friday-to-Monday parties at Taplow Court, Buckinghamshire (where M.B. was a frequent guest) and at Panshanger in Hertfordshire. She was for forty years the acknowledged hostess and main friend to M.B.'s elder brother John, 2nd Lord Revelstoke, devoted part of each week to his life and was chief mourner at his funeral in 1929. Thought to be the inspiration, in part, for the spellbinding Leila Bucknell, the Lesbia illa of M.B.'s *roman à clef C* (1922). M.B. wrote memorial poems to her elder sons Julian (author of *Into Battle*) and Billy who were killed in the war. She created their legend as precocious figureheads of a doomed generation in the privately published *A Family Memoir*.

Duff, Lady Juliet (1881–1965). The only child of the 4th Earl of Lonsdale, married Sir Robin Duff, Bt., in 1903. He was killed in action in 1914. They had one son, Sir Michael Duff. One of the most beautiful women of her generation, she was friends with many literary men, notably Belloc and Baring. M.B. wrote many letters to her, some of which were published in *Dear Animated Bust* (1981). In 1918 she married Major Keith Trevor and M.B. wrote;

> I've written plenty enough
> To Juliet Duff;
> I'll write nothing whatever
> To Juliet Trevor.

Gosse, Edmund (1849–1928). Poet, critic and man of letters; librarian to the House of Lords 1904–14; knighted 1925. He met M.B. at Arthur Benson's in July 1893 when M.B. 'thought indeed that never had I heard such intoxicating talk'. He dedicated his poetic fantasy *Hypolympia* (1901) to M.B. For further details of their friendship see *The Life and Letters of Sir Edmund Gosse* by Evan Charteris (1931).

Islington, Lady. Anne, daughter of H. Dundas of Dundas. Married 1895 John Poynder Dickson-Poynder, cr. Baron Islington 1910. M.B. dedicated *Diminutive Dramas* to her. She and he were supposedly in love as teenagers, when he knew her as 'Baabags'. He travelled to New Zealand in 1912 to stay with her while her husband was Governor General. She later became an ambitious hostess in a succession of grand houses.

L.C. This correspondent is unfortunately unidentified. The letters were returned to M.B. who carefully kept them.

'Lee, Vernon.' The pen name of Violet Paget (1856–1935), art historian, critic and novelist. Hon D.Litt (Durham) 1924. She lived in Florence and published scholarly Italian studies.

MacCarthy, Desmond (1877–1952). Critic, editor and author. Kt. 1951. Educated at Eton and Trinity College, Cambridge. Married Mary (Molly) Warre Cornish in 1906. During the Great War he served with the French Red Cross. He was a staunch supporter of M.B.'s writing, especially the mature novels of the 1920s.

Marsh, Edward Howard (1872–1953). Educated at Westminster and Trinity College Cambridge, where he was a scholar and was awarded the Senior Chancellor's medal for classics. He entered the civil service and, amongst many posts, was private secretary to Winston Churchill. He was a notable art collector, anthologist (*Georgian Poetry*), translator and author. His book *A Number of People* (1939) included a section on M.B. whom he met at Cambridge in 1893. C.M.G. 1908, C.B. 1918, C.V.O. 1922, K.C.V.O. 1937.

Maurois, André (1885–1967). Born Émile Herzog, French novelist, biographer and historian.

Orpen, William (1878–1931). Artist (official war artist 1917–19). K.B.E. 1918. R.A. 1919.

Smyth, Ethel Mary (1858–1944). Composer, author and feminist. A great friend and biographer of M.B. The first woman to compose large scale musical works. D.B.E. 1922.

Tatham, Mrs. Wife of Meaburn Talbot Tatham (1858–1937), who was educated at Eton and Balliol and taught at Rugby and Westminster before becoming a private tutor at Abingdon, where M.B. was immensely happy as a student in his house (see *The Puppet Show of Memory*). He and the Tathams made up triolets some of which were privately printed in 1893.

Trenchard, Hugh Montague (1873–1956). Entered Army 1893, D.S.O. 1906, Major-General 1916, Air Marshal 1919, Marshal of the Royal Air Force 1927. G.O.C. R.F.C. 1915–17. Chief of the Air Staff

1918–29. Commissioner Metropolitan Police 1931–5. Bt. 1919, Baron 1930, Viscount 1936, O.M. 1951. M.B. served on his staff in France and was best man at his wedding in 1920. His tribute to M.B. is included as an appendix.

Waugh, Alexander Raban (Alec) (1898–1981). Novelist. His book *The Loom of Youth*, based on a very frank description of his life at Sherborne School, became a best seller and caused his name to be erased from the school register. He later wrote a number of highly successful novels and other works of non-fiction. He served in the Army in both World Wars.

Wells, Herbert George (1866–1946). Author and sociologist. He and M.B. met at Lady Desborough's house, Taplow Court, at the beginning of the century and became lifelong friends. M.B.'s book *The Mainsprings of Russia* (1914) was dedicated to him.

Wilkinson, Henry Spencer (1853–1937). Fellow of All Souls and Chichele Professor of Military History (1909–23).

Woolf, Virginia (1882–1941). Novelist and critic. Daughter of Sir Leslie Stephen. Married Leonard Woolf 1912. A prominent member of the Bloomsbury Group.

HUBERT CORNISH   Florence
                                                            Tuesday, March 7, 93

My dear Hubs,

    ... I wonder if you have got any idea of the type of Florence; I had none before I came. The houses are very bright and are either white or yellow with green shutters... There are millions of narrow little streets ... with the deep burning sky in between their squalid and picturesque darkness. ... What I like best of what I have seen are Michael Angelo's statues of Night, Morning, Twilight and Dawn. ... Dawn seems to be struggling with the agony of intense weariness. And Night seems overwhelmed by an agonizing sleep. This statue is great and terrible with utmost despair; the very essence of 'I'm tired of tears and laughter',[1] but the sleep gained is not that of Proserpine's poppies. Two of [the statues] are very unfinished to me. It adds to the greatness of them that Michael Angelo with one or two blows has struck into them such potent life. Above the Dawn is a statue of one of the Medici; a man in armour, his head resting on one hand in thought. It is a figure that contains the whole strength of thought. ...

    I wish you could see Florence from a little terrace in the Boboli Gardens... It is the most magic place to look at, the white cathedral, Giotto's Campanile, the Palazzo Vecchio ... behind are the hills of Fiesole, very dark and soft sapphire blue in the afternoon but they grow purple towards evening. ... The sky remains blue at night, only instead of being made to turn and palpitate by the sun the moon makes it tremble with a darker and more mysterious azure. The air is charged with the smell of flowers now... I am employing all my spare time now in writing a short novel. I have finished about four or five chapters. It is giving me great pleasure. ...

    My ideas about Immortality are these. I believe in Immortality because I think it is contrary to reason and the laws of nature that one should go out like a candle. ... If you don't believe in a future life duty is

[23]

evidently absurd and pleasure is the only thing... Only I don't want to define it because I can no more understand it than I can eternity. If I can't understand and define this life that grasps at me every minute of the day still less can I understand or define a possible future one which I only believe in and have never seen.

Yrs, M.B.

1 Swinburne, 'The Garden of Proserpine'.

MRS TATHAM   Telegram sent 29 September 1893

Are you eating a goose?
It's the feast of St. Michael,
With stuffing and juice
If not you are loose
As regards the year's cycle.
Are you eating a goose
On the feast of St. Michael?

EDWARD MARSH   Hildesheim
                                                  [December, 1894]

Dear E.,

Is Stevenson dead or is he not?[1] There have always been so many rumours of his decease and Samoa is so far away that 'one really doesn't know what to think'.

I have been reading *La Débâcle* again.[2] I think some of it is as bad as any shilling shocker could possibly be; the descriptions of certain technical things where the technical words follow one another like the details of a pamphlet. The ambulance for instance. You suddenly feel as if a magic lantern slide was being put in for no reason except for brutal effect.

To say the sponge looked like a brain swimming about in the bloody pail is not good in any way. I always think my sponge looks like a brain when my nose bleeds – what else should it look like? Secondly it doesn't look in the least like a brain. To make an enormous picture, putting in every detail and by skilful tricks to persuade you that stuffed figures are part of the picture, that is called panorama, and Zola does it as well as it can be done. His distances are magnificent, some of the details

[24]

beautiful, the whole very fine and wonderful but the finest panorama is a million times a less great thing than a fine picture because it is a greater and more difficult thing to leave out than to put in. A more difficult thing [is] to give the effect of the whole by only showing a few parts than to overwhelm you with a sense of 'whole' by giving you all the parts. And as much as the best panorama is below a picture by Velazquez, Giorgione or Whistler so much is a book like *La Débâcle* below a work like *Macbeth*, *Phèdre*, *Fathers and Sons*, *Ghosts*, *Anna Karenina*. Don't think that I don't see how good *La Débâcle* is. I think that the part down to the end of Sedan [is] quite magnificent but the whole book is unleavened by any sense of humour. Between come bits where you feel the want of a sense of proportion, a sense of taste, bits which are badly written in a way that no great artist could badly write. The scene of the man being killed at the table is as bad as possible. And the evolution of Maurice's character! Childish!

Shopping before Christmas was like the scene of croquet in *Alice in Wonderland*; as soon as one found one's 'article' the attendant had disappeared; as soon as the attendant reappeared one could not find one's money; at last when one wanted to croquet the article with one's money, found and ready, and the attendant ready and waiting, someone else had bought and paid for the thing one had wanted.

Christmas week is a long procession of gloomy days here, like the procession of the ghosts of the kings in *Macbeth*, beginning with Christmas Eve, a spangled tinselled glittering king, ending with New Year's Eve, the Banquo, the ghost of murdered Christmas, a feeble monarch tottering under his broken crown, only kept alive by brandy.

Yours, M.B.

1 Robert Louis Stevenson (b. 1850) had died in Samoa on 3 December.
2 By Emile Zola (1840–1902), published 1892, dealing with the Franco-Prussian War and the Siege of Paris.

EDMUND GOSSE   Il Palmerino, Maiano, Florence
                                              17.2.96
Dear G.,
   I am staying with Vernon Lee for a week in her little villa which looks out on a wood with a Devonshire lane and a stream and has

behind it an endless stretch of corn-land and olive trees where one may walk and lie down as much as one pleases. ...

I have been to Paris where I saw a lot [of] plays and ate a lot of eggs, Oeufs à la Berg, Oeufs à la Mornay, Oeufs à la Polignac, Oeufs à la Grande Marnière, Oeufs à la Dame aux Camélias, Oeufs Trocadéro, Oeufs Néant, Oeufs à la vache espagnole, Oeufs à la Delamere Terrace, Oeufs Symbolistes, Oeufs Handschuhsheim, Oeufs au Rebours, Oeufs à la Melchior de Vogué.[1]

Then I went to Monte Carlo and basked in oranges and lemons and blue sea in a new white villa built in the style of Ouida and I won and lost at 30 et 40 till I had to run away to Florence where I have been ever since seeing strange people and delicate landscapes.[2]

Some of the people are certainly curious. For instance there is a family called Pieri Nerli, which you can read about in Dante's *Inferno*. Well, the surviving Nerli is what the Laureate would call 'unworthy scion of a noble race'.[3] And he found himself one fine day without a centime, literally. So he married a little wizened wicked old American damsel, aged 65 – imagine a small viper-like caricature of Lady Dorothy [Nevill][4] – who had £500 a year and wished to be called Pieri Nerli. The contract stipulated that he should receive clothes and food and £10 a year pocket money and that he should pay his wife three nightly visits a week.

What a lot of collectors there are in the world who are a disgrace to their cloth and calling. There is a certain Baron here who possesses a beautiful top-floor apartment which is pointed out by all Florence as the crown and glory of modern arrangement – 'such perfect taste and so comfortable'. It is one of those collections where everything is perverted from its original use with diabolical ingenuity. There is a dado of church vestments, a Venetian well for cigar ashes, a shrine picked up at Assisi for a letter box, *cassones* made into sofas and sofas made into chimney-pieces and, worst of all, bindings without books, bindings which enshrine spirit lamps to light cigarettes, bindings – beautiful bindings – out of which you pour out the tea! ...

I demonstrated in the streets the other day and shouted 'Abasso Crispi!'[5] and the soldiers came and the Colonel with tears in his eyes said to the crowd, 'Please be good and go home.' So we did. Gabriele D'Annunzio's latest work is full of exquisitely beautiful things; it is like a wonderful rhapsody of twilight music.[6]...

Yrs, Maurice

1 Of these various eggs, Polignac – a cold egg in jelly – and Mornay – in cheese – actually exist, but the rest are unknown to Gringoire and Saulnier's *La Répertoire de la Cuisine*. The Prince and Princess Edmond de Polignac were influential members of the literary and musical circle in Florence. *La Grande Marnière* was a novel (later dramatized) by Georges Ohnet (1848–1918). *La Dame aux Camélias* was a novel (1848) dramatized in 1852 by Alexandre Dumas fils (1824–95). The Palais du Trocadéro was built in Paris for the 1878 exhibition. Delamere Terrace was where Gosse lived. Schloss Handschuhsheim was the German residence of Harry Graham (1850–1933) at that time M.P. for West St Pancras; M.B. and Edward Marsh had both been guests there. *Au Rebours* (1844) was a decadent novel by Huysmans. Eugène Marie Melchior, Viscomte de Vogué (1848–1910), was a novelist and critic who specialized in Russian literature and was a member of the French Academy.
2 The 'Villa White' (Château Malet) where he stayed as the guest of Sir Edward Malet (1837–1908), a retired diplomat. See *The Puppet Show of Memory*. 'Ouida' was the pen name of Louise de la Ramée (1839–1908), an English novelist with a remarkably florid style.
3 Alfred Austin (1835–1913), poet laureate. The brief reference to Nerli is in *Paradiso* XI, 115, not *Inferno*.
4 Authoress (1826–1913), daughter of the 3rd Earl of Orford (of the second creation) and widow of Reginald Harry Nevill.
5 Francesco Crispi (1819–1901), Italian statesman of the left and follower of Garibaldi. Compelled to resign as premier in 1896 following the Abyssinian disaster of Adowa.
6 *Il Trionfo del Morto*.

EDWARD MARSH

Camacha
(or The Dank House)
St. Peter's Road
Bournemouth
13.8.97

My dear Eddy,

Thank you very much for letter and postcard, which I have not had the zeal to answer yet as I have to write business letters about Chilean forms and debentures and audit ale to stockbrokers nearly all day when I am adding figures for practice. I am improving in arithmetic, I think, which is a blessing.[1] First however your letterine. For a new boy I thought you didn't show enough respect and reverence for Bayreuth ... The astonishing thing about the scenery is not that it is good or bad but that it doesn't wreck the operas, as, for instance, the Lyceum Theatre scenery wrecks *Macbeth*. Perhaps you think it does? But surely the light effects are very fine and the church scene in *Parsifal*. I am all for its being Merg [German] and not French or Italian or Byzantine or Mauresque. Artists want the camellias and chameleons and 'sultan weeds' in *Parsifal* to be like the background of a primitif picture. I think it would be very much '*de côté*' and clash with the music. Other people want it to be Greek but there is no such mistake as mixing barbarian and Hellene. *Parsifal* is inarticulate, full of aspirations and religious yearning to the nth, which is the most Un-Greek thing in the world, isn't it? My authority is Renan and my own common-sense. ...

I wonder whether the second act of *Siegfried* was wonderful? And what was Donald Tovey like? ...

This is an English Timmes.[2] There are five daughters, one son, six pupils including myself. It is an enormous house. Rev A. J. Williams is the boss... He is very nice and good natured... He has got a wife who pecks about the room like a frightened hen. She is the most poopsy woman I have ever seen or heard. She asks my name nearly every day. She scarcely ever speaks, but every now and then she hazards a question like 'Do you think doctors look clever?' .... She is considered too incompetent to pour out tea and she <u>is</u>, because she doesn't know and can't learn the difference between tea and coffee, and milk and cream, and salt and sugar. One daughter is 'la femme incomprise', one is 'la femme forte', and one would like to be 'la femme aux hommes'. One is 'la femme qui ne se marche pas du pied comme une poule'.' The son is a curate.... I don't know which makes me grimmest. Of course he means to be awfully nice and fasts on Friday out of sheer gratuity. Why do curates get soap faced? He is very self satisfied. Now and then he talks with zeal and young enthusiasm about <u>we</u> and how disgraceful it is for people not to give more to the bag in church. This gives his father fearful kickscreams[3] and gives me untold pleasure just to put in a word agreeing with his father. The son then goes on talking <u>at</u> me on the same subject for the rest of the meal and I ignore him in serenity.

The other pupils are learned but very young, scarcely three years old. The food is disgusting. It is good on Monday, but it goes further than any food I have ever seen, and survives hash and grows into a curry. It not only changes in degree but in kind. Pork becomes mutton and beef becomes hare. It is very good for work. One gets up at 6.30! That is the type. The man can't do my difficult sums at all and has to get his daughter to do them, but that is exactly the man I wanted. He is worse at arithmetic than I am but by sheer industry accomplishes the work!....

Yours, M.B.

1 M.B. had failed the entrance examination for the Diplomatic Service owing to his complete inability to do arithmetic. At this time he was at a crammer's in Bournemouth. He failed in arithmetic again the following year but was given half-marks and passed because the French examiner went to the Board of Examiners and told them that his French essay might have been written by a Frenchman. At the time of writing he had already been to Bayreuth twice and had planned to go again with Marsh but had given his tickets to his friend Donald Tovey, (1875–1940), musician and scholar, who had become a friend at Oxford where he was music scholar at Balliol.

2 Dr Timmes was a tutor in Hildesheim to whom M.B. had been sent to learn German in 1892.

3 The Baring and Ponsonby families developed a private vocabulary. 'Kickscream' in Baring-Ponsonby language meant 'acute boredom; unbearable irritation'.

CECILIA WARRE CORNISH   Foreign Office
                                       November 17, 1898

My dearest Cecilia,

It is pitch dark from fog and I have got cramp in the middle figure of my right hand and so I can't write as long a letter as I meant to write to you this morning when I went to bed last night. I sent you a book called *The Traveller's Tale* – at least I told Mr Bain to send it you.[1] Did he? I then read it and found it was not at all a child's book though it looked like one. In fact that it was more suited for a stockbroker, a retired banker, or the directors of the South Western Railway. But I think it may amuse you all the same.

In a few days I shall send you a book of fairy tales, and when you have read that and if you are very naughty indeed and make Margaret cry and pinch Miss Weisse till she calls for a policeman, and if you adopt an impertinent tone to the Headmaster, and snub the Provost, and contradict Mr Rawlins twice, and strangle Mrs. Warre after pouring two sticks of boiling black sealing wax down her nostrils, and say 'How do you do' to Miss Copeman in Chapel, then I will send you a surprise box.[2]

Goodbye, or to put it more plainly as the Duchess said, Never imagine yourself not to be otherwise than what it might appear to others that what you were or might have been was not otherwise than what you had been would have appeared to them to be otherwise.[3]

Yours, M.B. S

S (that red S means that the letter has been seen by Lord Salisbury ...)[4]
Please write to me.

1 *A Traveller's Tale* after the Greek of Lucien de Samosate by Alfred J. Church, M.A., London 1880. James Bain, then in Haymarket, was a well-known London bookseller.
2 The people referred to were all Eton personalities. Miss Weisse was Dr Sophie Weisse (1851–1945), a German music teacher who taught Donald Tovey; Mr Rawlins was Francis Hay Rawlins (1850–1920), a notable classical scholar who was then an assistant master and who became vice-provost in 1916; Mrs Warre was the headmaster's wife; and Miss Copeman had been M.B.'s dame (matron).
3 Cf. *Alice in Wonderland* chapter 9.
4 The 3rd Marquess of Salisbury (1830–1903) was then prime minister and secretary of state for foreign affairs, hence M.B.'s supreme boss.

MRS CORNISH   British Embassy, Paris
                                               Saturday, March 4, 99

My dear Mrs Cornish,

I have never thanked you yet for your most charming letter. The most spoiling letter I have ever had in my life. I miss Eton dreadfully. 'Ille terrarum mihi praeter omnes', etc.[1] But this place is immensely interesting and exhilarating. I had influenza badly the night before last but there is something so recuperative in the atmosphere that I am about and practically well today. ... President Faure's funeral was a most beautiful pageant, starting at eleven in the morning; Paris was bathed in light and mist, 'all bright and glittering in the smokeless air'.[2]

The town looked as if it had just been made – 'When Paris like a mist rose into towers',[3] and every now and then you heard fragments of very soft military music, and a low mumbling of drums the whole time, and an intermittent booming of minute guns.

I walked behind four huge Germans, the four biggest men in Germany, whom the German Emperor, with that extraordinary delicate tact which he possesses, sent to remind the French of certain unpleasant facts. ... The service in Notre Dame was most magnificent, one organ answering the other, the most perfect orchestra and singing.

[30]

I don't know if you still take any interest in the Dreyfus case.[4] I fancy (although there is such a lull just now that you would think that no such case had ever existed) that when the Cour de Cassation[5] gives its decision there will be the most tremendous outburst – that is, if it is in favour of Dreyfus, as nine people out of ten have never taken that eventuality into consideration as being possible.

Waldeck Rousseau[6] made one of the most eloquent speeches ever spoken in the Senate the other day and the Senate only passed the bill from a wish not to add to the confusion. The ordinary Frenchman of the upper class you meet really in perfect sincerity looks upon 'Dreyfusards' as we look upon anarchists. They all have a profound belief in the infallibility of Courts Martial.

The infallibility of the Pope is a difficult doctrine for some people but the infallibility of seven officers! Good gracious! I won't bore you any more. Make one of your family write to me. I live for letters.

Yours most aff., M.B.

1 'That corner of the world smiles for me beyond all others.' Horace, *Odes*, book 2, no. 6.
2 From Wordsworth's sonnet 'Composed upon Westminster Bridge'.
3 Cf. Tennyson's 'Tithonus'.
4 The case of Alfred Dreyfus (1859–1935), an Alsatian Jew and an army officer, who was wrongly convicted in 1894 of selling French military secrets to the Germans, was referred to the United Appeal Courts by the Senate in February 1899 after a long campaign by his family and friends to prove his innocence. The case finally closed in 1906, the conviction being quashed. See *The Puppet Show of Memory*.
5 The Appeal Court.
6 Pierre Marie René Waldeck-Rousseau (1846–1904), French statesman and prime minister from 1899 to 1902.

MRS CORNISH   British Embassy, Paris
                                                              May 27,99
My dear Mrs Cornish,
My French parodies are going to be published next week ... I will send you a copy ... It is called *Hildesheim 4 Pastiches*[1]...

I am having such fun here now, and I've made the acquaintance of one of the nicest people I've ever seen, a Madame de Béarn,[2] a charming young woman with Anna Karenina eyes and the most beautiful house made of old Louis XIV *boiseries* and crammed with books, and she is most charming, nice and pointful, and infinitely intelligent. A confirmed Anti-Dreyfusard, which is such a good sign in France, as good as it is bad in England.

I went to the première of *Hamlet*[3] the other night ... you must be sure and see it. It is the ultimate triumph of intelligence, the victory over every obstacle of '*la matière*'. Sarah attempted the impossible and achieved it with ease ... I am reading Ruskin and *Les Évangiles* by Renan[4] in my spare moments.

Bless you all,

M.B.

1 M.B. wrote a note in the second edition (1924) that they were written '...more or less as a school exercise, when the author was cramming for a competitive examination in which French was an important subject'. They were shown by the British ambassador to a friend who showed them to the publisher Lemerre who published a small edition. The parodies were of Renan, Loti, France and Bourget and were dedicated respectively to his friends Hilaire Belloc, Hubert Cornish, Vernon Lee and Edmund Gosse.
2 Martine de Béhague (1869–1939), heiress and patron of the arts, with whom M.B. formed a friendship which he described as an '*amitié amoureuse*'. In 1902 he was to go in her yacht to Greece. She had made a disastrous marriage in 1890 to Count René de Béarn. They lived apart and she eventually resumed her maiden name. She inherited the Hôtel de Béhague in Paris (now the Romanian embassy) where she built the largest private theatre in Europe. While M.B. was in Russia in 1902 she arranged for his play *Gaston de Foix* to be translated into French to be read by Sarah Bernhardt in the hope of a performance with her as Gaston. When Baring had his portrait drawn by his niece Daphne Pollen in 1932 he gave her the original. Proust dubbed her his 'Delicious sauce Béarnaise'.
3 Sarah Bernhardt's production. See *The Puppet Show of Memory* and M.B.'s *Sarah Bernhardt* (1933) and *Punch and Judy* (1924).
4 Joseph Ernest Renan (1823–92), French historian and philosopher.

THE EDITOR OF THE *SATURDAY REVIEW*[1]   Paris

17th June, 1899

Sir,

Will you allow me to protest against the severe sentence passed by your brilliant dramatic critic ' Max', not on Sarah Bernhardt's interpretation of *Hamlet* but on the French language?

'The fact is', he states, 'that the French language, limpid and exquisite though it is, affords no scope for phrases which ... are charged with a dim significance beyond their sound. The French language, like the French genius, can give no hint of things beyond those it definitely expresses ... it is not, in the sense that our language is, suggestive. It lacks mystery. It casts none of those purple shadows which follow and move with the moving phrases of our great poets.' Surely this is merely equivalent to admitting (an admission which I have often heard made by Englishmen) that to him the French language is a vehicle merely. In English every word has its associations for us and touches off a train. Some words are enough in themselves to redeem a page; they are like men and women with identities, while French words seem to many of us and to 'Max,' according to the above quotation, to be like Noah's Ark men, merely symbols.[2]

But to the French and to those who imbibed the French language in their childhood words possess identity and association in the very same way.

I maintain that Racine's lines –

Ariane, ma soeur, de quel amour blessée,
Vous mourûtes aux bords où vous fûtes laissée! – [3]

are quite as suggestive as 'Rest, rest, perturbed spirit'.[4]

Or, to take other examples, Victor Hugo's

Vite, à tire-d'ailes! –
Oh! c'est triste de voir s'enfuir les hirondelles! –
Elles s'en vont là-bas vers le midi doré,[5]

or Baudelaire's

La Musique souvent me prend comme un mer vers ma pâle étoile,[6]

or Verlaine's

Au calme clair de lune triste et beau,
Qui fait rêver les oiseaux dans les arbres
Et sangloter d'extase les jets d'eau,
Les grands jets d'eau sveltes, parmi les marbres. [7]

All these phrases seem to me to have their mysterious shadows, their unearthly echoes. Matthew Arnold used to be fond of quoting a French Alexandrine couplet and immediately after a line or two of Shakespeare, and he would then exclaim 'What a relief!'

Yes, indeed, what a relief for an Englishman with an English ear but a Frenchman would invert the order of the quotations and say the same thing.

I admit that Shakespeare is a more suggestive poet than Racine, but surely this is not because French is a less suggestive language than English but because Shakespeare's genius and ideas were the more mysterious. On the other hand, the poetry of Villon, Ronsard, Victor Hugo, Musset, Baudelaire and Verlaine is to me every bit as suggestive as that of Sir Philip Sidney, John Donne, Wordsworth, Keats, Tennyson, and Mr. Swinburne.

I heard a German once say 'How poor your English language is! Instead of our beautiful word "Heimath" you have to say "Home", instead of "Mutter" you are reduced to saying "Mother". Ugh!'

This seems to me to put the matter in a nutshell; or perhaps a still better example is the old *Punch* story of the little girl who said to her nurse, 'And you must know, Parker, that in France they say Wee for Yes.' 'La! Miss,' answered the nurse, 'How paltry!' This is precisely the same sentiment as that expressed by 'Max', a sentiment against which I wish to protest.

I am, Sir, etc.

Maurice Baring

1 This letter, published on 24 June, gave rise to a lengthy and fascinating correspondence which was concluded by an editorial in the issue of 2 September. See *The Puppet Show of Memory*. In May 1898 Max Beerbohm had succeeded Bernard Shaw as dramatic critic. His notice of Sarah Bernhardt's *Hamlet* appeared on 17 June under the heading 'Hamlet, Princess of Denmark'. It was reprinted in *Around Theatres*.
2 This simile was used by Arthur Benson when he introduced M.B. to Gosse in 1893. See Evan Charteris, *The Life and Letters of Sir Edmund Gosse* (1931), p. 239.
3 *Phèdre* I, 3.
4 *Hamlet*, I, v, 182.
5 *Les Burgraves*.
6 'La Musique' in *Les Fleurs du Mal*.
7 'Clair de Lune' from *Fêtes Galantes*.

MAX BEERBOHM   British Embassy, Paris
                                                Saturday, June 17, 1899

My dear 'Max',

   (This is not meant as an impertinent familiarity: it is as if I wrote 'Dear
George Eliot'.) I have been greatly perturbed by your article on Sarah's
Hamlet: in fact I have unbosomed myself in a letter to the *Saturday
Review*. If they don't print it I wonder if you could get hold of it and read
it as I don't have time to write it all over again. It's not about Sarah's
interpretation that I quarrel with you (although I admired it immensely
and thought Sarah made a very good adolescent, a gentlemanlike boy,
very natural and sympathetic – moreover I thought it a triumph of intelligence over matter and sex and that the whole performance and
arrangement was saturated with the same intelligence). Where I revolt
is when you say that the French language can't be suggestive. But I argue
this fully in my letter to the Saturday which I hope you may see, and only
in the event of this hope proving to have been vain can I marshal my
arguments a second time and then it will be too late!

   I told Bain to send you a book of mine, or at least a tiny pamphlet.
I have enjoyed *More*[1] immensely and should like to see More and More.
Quoth the raven 'More and More'.

                                                Yours, Maurice Baring

1 Beerbohm had just published his book *More*.

MAX BEERBOHM   British Embassy, Paris
                                                Sunday, July 2nd, 1899

Dear 'Max',

   Thank you very much for your nice remarks about my letter to the
Saturday Review.

   I agree with you in thinking English more suggestive than French so
we needn't fight a duel, which would otherwise have been inevitable
(Gosse is my second, should the case recur) but you must remember
that you said that not only was English more suggestive than French
but that French couldn't be suggestive unless it was unintelligible:
whether suggestive[ness] increases with unintelligibility is another question (we neither of us think so) – the First Part of *Faust* is obviously
more suggestive than the Second – and I think that often the most lucid

[35]

prose of Maupassant and the most crystal verse of Racine have their purple shadows ...

Thank you again,

Yours, M. Baring

... I think English more suggestive than French because the English temperament has allowed it to leave more to the imagination, to be, as you said, a little more vague. But I think it is really because we are more imaginative, because the German language which is still more massive has not been allowed by the German poets to be as vague as English. What do you think? ... German words are, I think, as suggestive but German poetry is far less imaginative. I mean *The Ancient Mariner* and Keats and Shelley are really quite unintelligible to the German mind which likes its Pegasus in harness.

MRS CORNISH   British Embassy, Paris
                                               November 1, 1899

Dear Mrs Cornish,

I am going to the country to stay with Madame de Béarn's sister ... at a beautiful château called Courances.[1] ...

I am going again to *Tristan* tonight: the orchestra (Lamoureux) is wonderful. It is like a forest of wood-notes and a magic sea mixed. The singers are execrable; however they didn't attempt to sing so it didn't much matter.

I am going tonight with Madame Greffuhle.[2]

Yours, M.B.

1 A château near Fontainebleau owned by the Marquis de Ganay. Cf. *The Puppet Show of Memory*.
2 According to George Painter, in his *Marcel Proust, a Biography* (1959), the Countess Greffuhle was 'perhaps the most distinguished lady in the whole of Parisian society'. She was one of the main models for Proust's Duchesse de Guermantes.

MRS CORNISH   British Embassy, Paris
                        Friday, Nov. 3, 1899 (or Nov. 4 or 5)

Dear Mrs Cornish,

I came back from Courances on Wednesday evening, the day of ill

news:[1] 'they brought me bitter news to hear and bitter tears to shed'.[2]
The unkindest thing was I travelled up from Courances with a French officer, a violent nationalist; as we got into the train my eye caught the heading of defeat in the newspapers which I had bought at the station, so I stuffed them in my pocket and talked without drawing breath about musical chairs and Shakespeare till we arrived at Paris.

But the French as individuals, though they are very disapproving of the war – Dreyfusards to a man – are full of admiration for our soldiers, and are nice about it. Generals Négrier and Roget say that Gen. White was perfectly [right] in what he did, and that they would have done the same.[3]

Courances is a red brick Henri IV château surrounded by a great piece of water which makes a noise. It is in the middle of a Louis XVI park with shapely alleys, avenues, canals and ponds, and inhabited by exiled peacocks and discredited white pheasants; also by a tiny dog a square inch big called Hercule. The trees were like fire when I was there: golden torches for the funeral of the year.[4] 'Es mögen', I thought, 'die letzten Küsse des scheidenden Sommers sein.'[5]

We drove to Fontainebleau both afternoons through the dying forest which, like Mary Queen of Scots, had put on its most splendid clothes to die, and we visited the Château, which looked more beautiful and more completely sad than anything I have ever seen.

The dinners were very amusing. I never heard so much *relevage* in my life. We discussed Wagner and whether the greatest art required people to be educated in order to appreciate it, at the top of our voices, and I suddenly became conscious I was insulting an academician. The next night the officer and an ex-officer called Depré came to dinner, and M. de Ganay and M. Schlumberger,[6] welcomed the opportunity to talk about the Affaire which they had been longing to do, and so we plunged once more into that luring whirlpool, and I came out an uncompromising Anti-Dreyfusard, which I have long suspected that I was. The next night we discussed Napoleon's character till we were hoarse. ...

Yours, M.B.

1 The victory of the Boers outside Ladysmith.
2 From William Johnson Cory's (1823–92) 'Heraclitus'.
3 Field Marshal Sir George Stuart White (1835–1912) in command in Natal during the Boer War. Two courses of action were open to him: to attempt to check the Boer invasion of Northern Natal by holding first Dundee and then

Ladysmith; or deliberately to abandon those, hold the line of the Tugela River, and await attack in positions chosen for their purely strategic values. His stores, however, had accumulated at Ladysmith and he decided to defend it.
4 Cf. Pope 'To Mrs.M.B. on her Birth Day'.
5 Heine, quoted in M.B.'s *Algae*, his anthology of phrases (1928).
6 Jean Schlumberger (1877–1968), novelist and critic. One of the founders of the *Nouvelle Revue Française*.

EDWARD MARSH   British Embassy, Paris
                                          Saturday, December 16 [1899]
My dear Eddy,

I go to the Club sometimes and I have seen Madame de Béarn once or twice who is building the most beautiful Byzantine music room you ever saw, with an organ in it and a small stage with a hidden orchestra as at Bayreuth, where she is going to have played the plays thou wouldst have done and the music thou wouldst have played. There Louie Fuller is going to gyrate in circles of fire and there Rose Caron is going to appear in stiff tragic folds and tight-shut mouth.[1] There Sarah Bernhardt is going to walk across the stage dressed as a pope in silver and gold. ...

Yours, M.B.

1 Rose Caron (1857–1930) was a soprano diva of the Paris Opéra, Louie Fuller then a celebrated dancer.

EDMUND GOSSE   British Embassy, Paris
                                                    Dec. 29, 1899
My dear Chermaître,

A million blessings, a happy New Year and a trillion thanks for your letter which has just arrived.[1]

What you say about the poems is most encouraging and inspiriting, and makes me as proud as a pencilled peacock or Xmas goose. ... It is encouragement which is the only thing which makes one do anything at all, so it isn't bad for me! Twice for two years I entirely gave up all hope of ever writing anything at all and was really in a state of despair about it. Every now and then however there seems to be a sudden but short-lived sunbeam and then again the years of barrenness, the lean years of waiting. However they have now twice been interrupted by a tiny Spring when I had both times given up all hope whatsoever. So I hope it may happen again. In the meantime thank you.

Yes, it has been a melancholy Xmas but never have I been so proud of my country. Disasters and calamities which would throw France into revolution, Germany into Socialism, Russia into bankruptcy, merely brace the nerves of England and tighten its muscles. But oh! the lists of the killed and the gaps. ...

The other day there was a concert at the Ritz Hotel for the wounded in the Transvaal, in which all the best French singers took part, but the feature of the performance was Sarah B[ernhardt] who arrived looking old and worn in a fur coat. But she stepped on to the stage and recited to an accompaniment on the piano Victor Hugo's lovely and exquisite lyric, 'La Chanson d'Eviradnus' in *La Légende des Siècles*, which begins,

> Si tu veux faisons un rêve,
> Montons sur deux palefrois;
> Tu m'emmênes, je t'enlève,
> L'oiseau chante dans les bois,

and all at once she was transformed and transfigured and before us in the stuffy concert-room floated a vision of mysterious wood-ways, of dew-drenched grasses, whispering leaves and notes and flutes and startled cries, and a scent of spring, and the sap and the breeze of youth as her words rippled on like drops of dew in a crescendo of ecstasy. In the front row there was a picked and blasé audience if ever there was such a thing and they were all in tears and all saying: 'What a marvellous Woman.' ...

The Mexican Minister, who was buried in Xmas Week, had a funeral tinged with festivity – a soupçon of Xmas... An enormous chest of drawers draped in black and silver had been erected in the middle of the church; on the top of this a plum pudding with a sprig of holly floated in flaming spirits of wine while around it arranged symmetrically were twelve burning mince pies. Round the base of the chest of drawers was a kind of rampart of black cotton wool in which the servants of the deceased were imbedded with the heads protruding, the idea being that they should be nearest to the remains. They looked, however, weary of this nestling and nesting for we all had to wait – we in uniform – an hour while the organ was being tuned. Then when the corpse was brought one of the drawers of the chest of drawers was opened and it was flung in and the drawer locked up. ...

Yours aff., M.B.

1 M.B. had sent Gosse a copy of his *Poems*, privately printed by the Cambridge University Press in 1899. This letter is in reply to one from Gosse, included in Evan Charteris, *The Life and Letters...* (*op. cit.*), on pp. 267–9: ' ...*Altera Circe* is the only piece I had not seen before. It is extremely melodious and delicate. The last line is like a sea-scape on a Japanese fan. I like the old sonnets more and more, *La Calice* is without question one of the most beautiful sonnets of our age. It is absolutely perfect, not a flaw in it from first to last...'

EDWARD MARSH   British Embassy, Paris
                                                   January 8th, 1899 [*sic*]
Eddy my dear,

Was it you sent me the telegram about Ladysmith? If so bless you with all my heart. All day long there have been rumours that Ladysmith had fallen. Everybody thought so here apparently except me. ...I was pining for news when a telegram came and the relief was intense. ...You can't think how short of true news one is here. ...

Americans are sadly lacking in *le sentiment de la mesure*. I had luncheon at [the] Ritz Hotel with the American Minister at Rio. It was a luncheon given to Brazilian Ministers at Paris – five dingy, darkling diplomats. ... The table was banked with roses, lilac, mignonette and pink carnations and a cuckoo sang in a recess of marigolds. A fountain of Jockey Club scent soared from a silver pond in which were real nautili. The vista of wine glasses was interminable and kaleidoscopic in effect of colour – red, blue and white. ... And in front of every guest was a bouquet of extinct orchids. The very hors d'oeuvres were great auk's eggs and one felt one was cheating the British Museum in eating them. Then came the spoils of Russian lakes and Norwegian fjords, the spices of the West Indies, the Urim and Thummim (an American dish), and the terrapin (an American dish likewise). And the juvilas of humming-birds and the larynxes of nightingales and a Welsh Mammoth.

It was almost a waste as the guests were following a strict régime and were only allowed to eat stale bread and drink mineral waters. So I had to eat most of it and I haven't been the same since. ... By the way towards the end of this astounding meal the healths of every magnate in Brazil were drunk in a religious undertone.

Goodbye,

yrs, M.B.

EDMUND GOSSE British Embassy, Paris
21.1.1900

My dear Chermaître,

How nice of you to send a letter to bring kindly light amid the encircling gloom.

Rain and rumours of disaster and defeat envelop this city. The news seems better; but I live in terror of opening the morning paper.

Cheerfulness however as you say breaks in. I have nothing much to tell you except that I made the acquaintance of Sarah B. ... I sent her printed *à un exemplaire* the little masterpiece of Victor Hugo she recited at the concert in aid of the British wounded; she professed herself highly touched; we sobbed in each other's arms in her sitting room at the theatre which is like the white satin railway carriage in which Queen Victoria travels.

How amusing your meeting Lady Kenmare.[1] She is an entertaining creature from the dramatic point of view. If you are nice to her and give in she will be charming to you but she is the most autocratic of egoists. However she has imperial ideas, artistic instincts and infallible taste, much culture, much knowledge, a fine capacity for telling lies, intense extravagance, no money but a genius for making bricks without straw, and considerable generosity and unbounded hospitality. She should have been a courtesan in the reign of Louis XIV. (Very confidential.)

I have been gloating over Stevenson's letters.[2] I have also made the acquaintance of a most charming Frenchman called Chevrillon who wrote a celebrated article on Kipling in the *Revue de Paris*, which was remarkable for an analysis of the English character in general.[3] ...You must make his acquaintance.

Have you read Ibsen's play? It is very heady, full of atmosphere and such a strange atmosphere but I am told that the French translation which I read is most inadequate.[4]

I am very tired. We had a farewell dinner to someone who is going away and I sang or rather improvised songs in German, French, Italian, American, Boer and bandesrath till a late hour in the morning.

I suppose Lord Methuen will be carried in triumph to the lunatic asylum on his return.[5]

Write to me,

Yours ever, M.B.

1 (1840–1913), wife of the 4th Earl, and mother-in-law to M.B.'s sister Lady Castlerosse.
2 Stevenson's *Letters to His Family and Friends*, edited by Sidney Colvin, 1899.
3 André Chevrillon (1864–1957), man of letters and critic. Author of *Études* (1910) and *Nouvelles Études Anglaises* (1910) and *Kipling* (1903). His studies helped greatly in introducing contemporary English writers to the French. He was a nephew of Taine.
4 The Norwegian playwright's work was especially admired by M.B. The play referred to was presumably *When We Dead Awaken*.
5 Paul Sanford Methuen, 3rd Baron (1845–1932). Later field marshal, as a lieutenant-general commanded 1st Division in South Africa. His attack on Magersfontein in 1899 had miscarried, but the criticisms levied against him at the time have since been considered unjust.

MRS CORNISH   British Embassy, Paris
                                                Feb. 7, 1900

My dear Mrs Cornish,

Today after weeks of rain the glorious sun uprist and bathed Paris in dazzling whiteness. I went for a long walk on the quays and bought a History of the Vandals and a Racine, 25 cents each. I had an hour's conversation with my bookbinder as he worked on a stool at the most elaborate bit of mosaique work, inlaying tiny bits of crimson Morocco in gold fleurs-de-lys, while his wife from the next room threw in desultory remarks about the pity of it that I was so unsound about margins, insisting as I do in invincible ignorance on not having them *rogné* and *doré sur tranches*. We talked about millionaires and their ignorance and about bibliophiles and their angelic sweetness and about big books and small books and vellum *doublures* and *ciseléd* leaves. People were working all round and at the end Mercier's wife ran and fetched the Livre de Messe her husband had bound for her wedding; such an elaborate binding has never been seen. It had every flower in the Garden of Eden and every colour in the rainbow and every device of heraldry: it was a piece of sheer *bravoure*, like Melba's roulades in *Lucia* or like Sarasate when he plays *Au Claire de la Lune*, if he ever does.[1]

Hilaire Belloc was here on Sunday, more subdued than usual and less truculent. We went to the Louvre and to the Concert Rouge and to Vespers at St. Sulpice and to Benediction at Notre Dame, and then for a long long drive on the top of an omnibus during which Hilaire pointed out to me Danton's house and Danton's prison and Danton's café and Danton's theatre and Danton's chapel and Danton's tennis court and Danton's 'Kegelbahn' and Danton's tobacconist.[2] I daresay he didn't know anything about it but I have the faith that swallows archaeologists. I have still got bronchitis but am quite well.

What a wonderful book *The Mill on the Floss* is! How intensely poetical – the epic of childhood, with its mystery and awe and moments of misery. I think she knew Stephen Guest was what he was.

Yrs, M.B.

1 Nellie Melba (née Mitchell) (1861–1931), Australian prima donna, D.B.E. 1918, G.B.E 1927. Pablo de Sarasate (1844–1908) Spanish violinist and composer. 2 Joseph Hilaire Peter Belloc (1870–1933), poet, historian, essayist and novelist. M.B. met him at Oxford and they became firm friends. In 1899 he published his life of Georges Jacques Danton (1759–94), French revolutionary politician.

MRS CORNISH

British Embassy, Paris
February 22, 1900

My dear Mrs Cornish,

I went to see Anatole France[1] this morning. ... It was most amusing. There was an extraordinary collection of people, ex-Governors of Colonies and young students with beards and big ties. One of them was a very young and very violent *anti-militariste*. He said the Boer War was a crime just as the French expedition to Madagascar had been and any army was a criminal thing. I told him I thought wars and armies were necessary evils and inevitable if painful results of human nature. At the end of our conversation he said: 'Je vous demande pardon de la brutalité de mes sentiments.' I said: 'Pas du tout, Monsieur. Je vous demande pardon de la douceur des miens.' ...

Good bye,

Yours aff., M.B.

1 Pseudonym of Jacques-Anatole Thibault (1844–1924), French novelist.

HILAIRE BELLOC   [British Embassy, Paris]
                                                   15 March 1900

My dear Hilaire,

I wish you would write an article in *The Speaker* to this effect on Anglo-French relations.

1a There is a widespread impression in France that as soon as war is over in [South Africa] England will attack France.

1b No responsible person in France nor the mass of the people wishes for war with England.

2a There is a widespread impression in England that as soon as the exhibition[1] is over France will attack England.

2b The mass of English do not want war with France. If any responsible people do it is because they base their opinion on the conviction that France wants war with England.

From this two conclusions:

1 That it is a reciprocal *malentendu* and the sooner it is dissipated the better.

2 The only persons who would profit from such a war would be the Germans who are doing as they have always done everything they can to bring it about.

This would come at a very opportune moment; vide today's *Times*.

                                                   Yours, M.B.

1 The Paris International Exhibition of 1900.

MRS CORNISH   [British Embassy, Paris]
                                                   March 17, 1900

My dear Mrs Cornish,

I must write you a line about the first night of *L'Aiglon*[1] to which I went.

The theatre was paved with beaten celebrities. The Dreyfusard sat next to the Anti-Dreyfusard, the Jew next to the Nationalist. The dress circles glittered with intelligent eyes and the boxes were elegant with stupid beauty and consummate toques.

Sarah's *entrée* was glorious. It was difficult to believe she wasn't Napoleon's son. She looked 17, fresh, young, slight and manly, and soon the electricity of her personality got the audience into a state of delirium.

All the epic of Napoleon was in her eyes. The play is, I think, very
fine, an *épopée*, more human than *Cyrano* and on a higher level altogether, though less finished, compact and coherent. The verses the same
type but, I think, more serious. Better, of course, as in *Cyrano*, to hear
than to read.

Life seemed to fade the next day after this bit of history which was
like a looking-glass to a larger history.

I forgot to say that in the entr'acte of *L'Aiglon* I went and kissed
Sarah's hand. In her *Loge* were Sardou, Anatole France, Duc de Rohan,
Reinach, Hervieu, Coquelin and many others. ...

Yours, Maurice

1 The play was first produced at the Théâtre Sarah Bernhardt on 15 March
with Sarah as L'Aiglon. M.B.'s review was republished in *Punch and
Judy*.

MRS CORNISH Paris, Day after Mi-Carême, 1900
March 23

My dear Mrs Cornish,

Yesterday morning I went to see Anatole France again in his high
mediaeval cell.[1] Jaurès, the Socialist,[2] was there, talking with rich flow
of language and a Gascon accent, and in the corner observing the
cobwebs was M. Emile Zola. Anatole France didn't like *L'Aiglon*.
Unfortunately it has been made a political question and as the Anti-
Dreyfusards have adopted it, the Dreyfusards feel obliged – and are
convinced as they say so – to say that it is worthless. Suddenly, however,
he put Aeschylus on the block and talked for half an hour in the most
brilliant and subtle way about this author, who is happily out of reach
of the Dreyfus affair. I, for one, was intoxicated by *L'Aiglon*, be it good
or bad. I think there is room in the music of the world for the band of
brass instruments and fifes and drums skilfully playing inspiriting
martial themes, as well as for the Schumann quintet and the Kreutzer
Sonata.

Rostand has got by instinct what Ibsen learned after being a stage
manager for many years and what Shakespeare as an actor must have
known and realised, the *doigté du dramaturge*, an incomparable
instinct for stage effect and appreciation of the value of the footlights.

And what to me is his greatest charm is that he is a poet who has deliberately taken a poetical view of existence and woven his dreams and built up fabrics of fantasy and blown enchanted soap-bubbles for the joy of it: he has no mission, no purpose: he brings no 'pageant of a bleeding heart',[3] he does not seek the cosmic significance of modern life, including the telephone, nor has he come as physician to probe the wounds of his generation, but every now and then in the cycle of humanity it is necessary that an irresponsible singer should come and say in spite of much opposition that there are many beautiful things in the world and that it is good that someone should re-tell the old story which it is not thought worth-while to repeat – the old story of Spring and Summer, of Hero and Leander, of Romeo and Juliet, of Captains like D'Artagnan, Kings like Henry V, Emperors like Napoleon, Knights like Bayard and Bussy, Soldiers like Ney and Lannes, Queens like Cleopatra and Marie Antoinette, and sing the losing side, chant a golden optimism in spite of evidences and appearances to the contrary, fight for impossible causes and resuscitate faded romances. This Rostand has done and whatever may be the merit of his poetry, his lines have often the smell of spring flowers and often the sound of pipes and bells and golden harps. Dieu Merci.

I am writing this letter in trying circumstances: a poodle who I am sure contains in him Mephistopheles is skipping on the writing tables and barking all the time: five people are talking: one person is type-writing, *qui est ennuyeuse chose à ouir.* I am reading Froissart and Shakespeare. Anatole France was in Windsor last week: he wrote to me for a permission to visit the State Apartments. I wrote to Fritz,[4] but it was too late.

I am, with love to all,

Yrs, Maurice

1 In *The Puppet Show of Memory* M.B. wrote: 'I made acquaintance with Anatole France and attended some of his Sunday morning levées at the Villa Said in the Bois de Boulogne. When I first went there, I never heard any topic except *L'affaire* mentioned, and indeed the only people present at these meetings were fanatical partisans of Dreyfus who did not wish to talk of anything else.'
2 Jean Jaurès (1859–1914). Founded *L'Humanité*. Assassinated.
3 'What helps it now, that Byron bore...The pageant of his bleeding heart?' Matthew Arnold, 'Stanzas from The Grande Chartreuse'.
4 Col. the Rt. Hon. Sir Frederick Ponsonby.

HUBERT CORNISH   Copenhagen
                                            10th August, 1900

My dear Hubertine,

This is a Hildesheim. I feel I ought to be at the Timmes; *les moeurs danoises* are very simple; the King of Denmark meets one at the station and carries your luggage on his back to the hotel.

I had a very wonderful journey here but I was horribly disturbed on the steamer by a Dane in an Alpaca ulster and spectacles, shooting a stuffed wild duck in the cabin next to mine all night. When I arrived the British Fleet were sailing up the Sound and bombarding the capital, which was tumbling to pieces like a child's brick castle.

It is dark and raining and the climate makes one feel as if one had no bones at all and makes one's nerves sing so that you feel like Nietzsche and *Hedda Gabler* mixed but after a day I believe you feel gloriously well and wake up as Hereward the Wake.

I am going to take two delicious rooms with a stove and a sofa and a spare room for you to come and stay in; you must. I have already read more in the last day and a half than in the last two years. I miss you all very much but I feel as if I was in Heaven ... *Il faut beaucoup aimer la Danemark* is my new motto and *beau comme un danois* is my new phrase. ...

I have been reading a book by Maupassant and knocked down by his extraordinary mastery of his art and his tools.

                                            Sincerely, M.B.

EDWARD MARSH   British Legation, Copenhagen
                                                    [no date]

My dear Eddy,

....Copenhagen is the noisiest capital under the sun. It is a place full of colour and subtle purity. I am bird happy....

It has one incurable lacuna, no type-writers in the Legation. My heart harks back to Remington.

> Come back to Remington,
> Come to the keys
> (O type-writer, my type-writer).
> Come back to Remington
> Under the trees.

This is the type here:

8 a.m. Called by a Danish Mädchen, who comes trilling into the room, singing a wild snatch about Kugl and Flugl and then breaks into a Gögel.

8, 1 second. I wake up.

8.20 I get up and wash Dr. Saboureau's tar off my head.[1] This takes 40 minutes.

9–9.15 dressing.

9.30 A Danish breakfast is brought in by the Mädchen. The table is covered with small bits of bread and butter. It is a rule in Denmark that whatever the meal the table must be covered.

10 I trudge to the legation. Olaf the Dane, the Chancery servant, opens the door: he is a 'knurd' in the morning but sobers towards sunset. He has whiskers, white fair hair and a child's blue eyes. He tells one exactly what to do, wear and say, and sends you home if you haven't got a blueface tie on.[2]

10–1 p.m. A period on my part of faintness, bodily faintness amounting to nausea and paralysis from hunger, during which the work of the Chancery is done. I docket, enter, register, minute, draft, copy out and put away. Goschen[3] directs from a room at the top of the house this perfect machine. The work is exiguous but I do it all. Goschen looks like a sailor: like the captain of a man-of-war: blue serge, a beard, square and thick, blue eyes... In fact, he is delightful. He plays the violin by himself, and has bought a small sailing yacht, and has an intense *culte* for Marryat and Fenimore Cooper.[4]

1 o'clock. Luncheon at restaurant with Goschen. A Danish luncheon proper consists entirely of hors d'oeuvres on a large scale. The table is littered with smoked and smelt raw salmon, live trout, dead whiting, black eel, seal, potted seal, roast seal, boiled seal, flat seal, green seal, herring, herring bones, herring stitches, shrimps, crayfish, cucumber, anchovy, Norwegian anchovy, bloater, bloater paste (*raffinistes Zeug*), pickles, leeches, leeks, onions, salads, mayonnaise, sauce, jelly, slips of sausage, tinned apricot, tinned bilberries, tinned blueberries, tinned holly berries, tinned holly, tinned mistletoe, tinned plum-pudding, tinned Christmas trees, tinned mince-pies, tinned snapdragon, tinned biltong, tinned bullybeef, tinned Olive Schreiner, tinned De Wet, tinned Baden Powell, tinned Rhodes, tinned Dreyfus, tinned Ibsen, tinned Bjornson, tinned Nell Gwynne, tinned Nelson.

But you see, when one says that luncheon consists mainly of hors d'oeuvres, it sounds very little but when one comes to think of it, it is a great deal. For those who dislike *Les Mélanges*, it is a poor look out. ...

After luncheon the midnight sun sets and the Aurora Borealis spreads over the sky and shooting stars leap and dance. We go out; I have a Danish lesson at 2, but the last three days we have had to go to Fredericksborg every day to write our names on the Empress of Russia, or receive the Princess of Wales, or write our names on the Princess of Wales, or on the King of Greece, or on the Crown Prince of Denmark. In a nest of Princes I hid my heart. There are Princes here, Princes there, Princes everywhere, Princes in the mountain, Princes in the glen. We went down to receive the Princess of Wales the day before yesterday. She arrived at nine and we stood in top-hats and frock-coats on the tiny platform, while six pensioners, all with wooden legs and hooks for hands and one eye, all wounded at the bombardment by Nelson, stood near us, and then a man arrived, dressed in a long black dressing-gown which reached to his feet and a long white ruff round his neck and a hat like this [drawing of a high, pointed hat]: at first I thought it was Queen Elizabeth and then I thought it was Cagliostro[5] and then an Inquisitor: but he turned out to be the Court Clergyman, who had come to read the service for those in the train, but as he didn't get there till the train arrived, the service had to be changed to the service for those at a station. The royalties descended to the platform and kissed the King, who up to then had been kept in a small waiting room with a chandelier to make it royal and then after a great deal of *grusse* they drove off. Then the Royal Mattress had to be made into a parcel, and when this had been done, the Danish Army, which was all of it there and consists of forty generals, twenty-five officers, ten sergeants and five men, lifted it and carried it to the slot (or glot?), which is Danish for castle. ...

Yours, M.B.

British <u>Legation</u>, please, not <u>Ministry</u>!!! I blushed when I got your letter, it looked as if you thought the British Legation was a Wesleyan Society for reforming the Danish Royal Family.

1 A hair restorer that did not work.
2 In Baring-Ponsonby language, one who has seen an unpleasant sight.

3 William Edward Goschen (1847–1924). At that time Envoy Extraordinary and Minister Plenipotentiary at Copenhagen. Later ambassador at Vienna and Berlin. G.C.V.O. 1904, P.C. 1905, baronet 1916.
4 Frederick Marryat (1792–1848) and James Fenimore Cooper (1789–1851), both of whom wrote popular adventure stories for boys.
5 Count Alessandro di Cagliostro (1743–95), charlatan.

EDWARD MARSH   British Embassy, Copenhagen
                                                December 16th, 1901
Beloved Eddy,
    ...Ethel Smyth visited this town about three weeks or a month ago. It was very exciting. Her new opera, *Der Wald*, has been accepted by the Berlin Opera for February next. Will you come and hear it? I invite you. Do you remember our breakfast in Charles Street [when] she told us the story of it? It is the same story and the music is exceedingly beautiful, at least I think so. I discovered all by myself the other day the Fifth Symphony of Beethoven. I went away another man. I like it infinitely better than the Eroica. Ethel tells me I am right and that it is to the Eroica as a Himalayan range is to a beautiful Welsh valley. ...

                                                Yours, M.B.

REGINALD BALFOUR   British Embassy, Rome
                                                Thursday, July 17, 1902
My dear R.,
    ...I have gone back to my old idea, that one must be born a R.C. to be one – only there are other things as well. At the same time I wish I had been born one. But nothing can make me believe if one is a Christian that it can be a matter of life and death which church one belongs to... I don't even see the necessity of belonging to any church and do not see why one shouldn't be a Christian 'la Bible à la main'. ... The church as manifested at Rome affects me neither one way nor the other. I think its manifestations here deplorable but that does not affect its eternal claims. ...

                                                Yours, M.B.

British Embassy, Rome
                                            2 August, 1902

My dear Simpaticissima Miss Paget,

It was a very great pleasure to get your letter which brought
the smells of a forest, a German Wald on an Italian hill, to Rome.
…

The fact remains that I prefer Swinburne to Browning, Rossetti and
many others and in making Gepäcks[1] you must have what Countess
Benckendorff calls no 'respect humain' and only suit your taste. I seek
no intellectual or very little intellectual pleasure in poetry; I like there
to be some 'fundamental brainwork' but in Browning there seems to
me, with the exception of about a dozen lyrics, one or two passages of
blank verse and single lines scattered all through his work, fundamental brainwork and nothing else. What I want is the 'Muse's
madness' and, short of actual frenzy, strong emotion, so strong that it
bursts into song and changes the words into gold and adds a fourth
indefinable dimension, 'not a third sound but a star'. I wish poetry to
affect me as music does, only to be articulate. I don't care twopence
for chiseled masterpieces of form, for exquisite impeccability.
Théophile Gautier, Leconte de Lisle, Richepin leave me cold; they
amuse but do not ravish me.

Musset with all his faults carries me away. I don't mind the
longueurs and the lapses, the twigs in the current, as long as the river
is there, full, swirling, seething, coming from some mysterious mountain, going to some undiscovered sea. Well, with Swinburne I am
convinced that in the work of his best early period you are face to face
with such a river, in *Atalanta* and poems like 'The Triumph of Time'.
I think he is inferior to Shelley, Keats, Milton, Heine, Leopardi in the
same way as Wagner is inferior to Schubert and Schumann and Bach
and Mozart. … I think Swinburne attained certain effects by certain
mechanical processes. [But] I think you get many manifestations of
unmistakeable genius, poetry, inspiration, muse's madness, just as you
do in *Tristan*, *The Meistersinger* and portions of *Walküre*, and
Siegfried which one cannot help admitting, anti-Wagnerian tho' one
may be and tho' I am.

But just as one may sometimes like to plunge into Wagner's domin-
ion where you never rise on wings into the heaven of heavens but
drown in ecstasy in a heavy sea, so sometimes I like to plunge into

Swinburne and revel in the heady sound and the sumptuous imagery. At such times poems like 'The Triumph of Time' (tho' it is much too long) with the recurrence of lines such as

> I had grown pure as the dawn and the dew
> You had grown strong as the sun and the sea –

or

> There lived a singer in France of old
> By the tideless dolorous midland sea.
> In a land of sand and ruin and gold
> There shone one woman, and none but she,
> And finding life for her love's sake fail,
> Being fain to see her, he bade set sail,
> Touched land, and saw her as life grew cold,
> And praised God, seeing, and so died he –

or the end of the poem which so transported Ethel, 'Anactoria', satisfy me as nothing else does. When one says these things are too long, if they weren't too long they wouldn't exist.

Of poets who pour out this volume of music you have a quantity and they write impeccable sonnets which bore me.

And now I am going to contradict myself because I think the same thing applies to Browning: his *longueurs,* his grotesque diction I know to be equally indispensable but I haven't inside me the seidlitz powder which, when mixed with Browning, produces combustion and this is my misfortune and not Browning's fault.

I remember you saying that in the 'Grammarian's Funeral' every line was bad and the whole splendid and that it was like Shelley's 'Cloud' in that respect, but the whole of Shelley's 'Cloud', if you read it aloud, carries you away by its music and in every line almost there is a magnificent image. ...

I have got leave and am going next week to Russia to stay with the Benckendorffs. Do write to me there. ...

Yours affect., Maurice

1 Literally 'baggage' but used by M.B. to denote the anthologies he made for many years, binding together pages cut from books of poetry. Several were given to his friends. He published one anthology, *Have You Anything to Declare?* (1936), and the anthology of phrases, *Algae* (1928).

Eddy,

... I must tell you something about Vernon. In practice she is like you; she can only read Shelley and even Milton in fragments, no French poetry at all. I think why she likes Browning so much is that it is indistinguishable from prose. ... Here I state for no reason at all that personally I think both kinds necessary, I mean Parnassians and the opposite.[1] I want Pope and Byron, Racine and Musset, Herédia, Tennyson and Walt Whitman.

Brewster, with whom I talked over the matter briefly a few days ago, said he thought both things were necessary; he considered one had the right to look at sonnets closely with a microscope and require them to be impeccable but that one should look at a play further off and judge it more as one judges a human being. There I agree. ...

My experience of the effect of years on my palate is that I like a far fewer number of poets, only more intensely. I like Milton, Keats, Shelley, Marlowe, Heine, Shakespeare, Dante, Victor Hugo and Musset more intensely than when I was 18 but others I liked then I can scarcely read at all, such as the whole of Rossetti, with [the] exception of a few fragments, Browning, except a few fragments, and a myriad smaller ones.

One I have annexed, Byron, whom I used to spew. I find if you read him – at least if I read him – by quantity, not looking close, and a lot at a time, I feel that I am reading poetry – real poetry.

I have met two people who seemed to me to judge people and things in Space. One is my Russian friend, Countess Benckendorff, who does so being a child of nature and because her feelings and thoughts come rushing out like a spring out of a rock with incredible force and freshness, and the other is Brewster, who seems to have floated through the world, his personality shielded by a thin, invincible armour of haze which has kept him from the influence of his fellows. ...

Yours, M.

1 M.B. wrote in *French Literature* (pp. 70–1): 'The romantic movement is said to have come to an end in 1860... Then came the so-called Parnassians, pessimists in outlook and obsessed with a passion for form.' He then mentioned Leconte de Lisle, Sully, Prudhomme, François Copée, Héredia, and Charles Baudelaire.

MRS CORNISH [Rome]
December 12th, 1902

My dear Grandmamma,

I would like to soar over in a balloon and drop into the warm darkness of the Cloisters. It seems to me centuries since I was in England.
...

Last night I dined at the house of a Countess Levatelli, an Italian woman of the 18th century who has taken a German degree at Göttingen in palaeontology and has a library and a salon, a cat and a tame buffoon, and the salon is full of the most incongruous elements, archaeologists, Germans, soldiers, Swedes, diplomatists, foreigners. Last night there were ten Germans at dinner and Monsignor Duchesne, the head of the French archaeological school.[1] ...

Yours, Petitfils

1 Louis Marie Olivier Duchesne (1843–1922), prelate, scholar and writer; one of the most distinguished religious historians of the nineteenth century. He became director of the École Française de Rome in 1895.

EDMUND GOSSE [Rome]
19 Sept. 1903

My dear Amico della Mandola,

I am leaving for Russia tomorrow morning to begin my well-earned leave. I am going to the Bencks. Heinemann is now brooding over translations of Gogol. ... I have talked with John.[1] John feels I must settle the matter myself and he would acquiesce in the idea of my leaving the F.O. if I can find work which would bring a certain remuneration. ... My sister Margaret thinks I am quite right and is convinced that if I stay in the F.O. I would never write another line; it is too physically exhausting. ... I cannot help thinking that with the certainly despicable trick I have of fastening on to the meaning of foreign languages I ought to be able to make some practical use of it.
...

Yours with blessings, M.

1 M.B.'s eldest brother, John (1863–1929) who had succeeded as 2nd Lord Revelstoke in 1897.

VERNON LEE   Sosnofka, Tambov, Morshank, Russia, via Moscow
                                    October 14–15–16–17? 1903

My dear Miss Paget,

... What you say about impatience at the charming idle people who cultivate feeble tastes interests me and stirs up many dormant thoughts.[1] I do <u>not</u> share your impatience for reasons which I will try to explain.

Firstly, it seems to me it is the very existence of such people that enables the thorough and industrious class to work and exist at all.

Renan says somewhere, in his *Dialogues Philosophiques*, I think, that if there were not a multitude of people going to the Auteuil races he would not be sitting in his *cabinet de travail* at work; that 10,000 idle people are necessary in order that one savant may work. ... By eliminating these idlers it seems to me you would disturb the economy of nature. ...

Secondly, Renan says somewhere else in reference to Petronius Arbiter, *n'est pas roi de la mode qui veut* and that the world would lose if it were composed merely of *des loudauds pédants*... I think that the existence of merely frivolous people who are bent on amusement is a necessary element in this grey world and that Helen of Troy, Mary Stuart, Ninon de l'Enclos, Diane de Poitiers, Petronius Arbiter and Charles II are equally necessary to the scheme of things as St. Paul, Thomas Aquinas, Marcus Aurelius, John Knox, Pym and Lady Jane Grey, whom we appreciate all the more by reason of contrast.

Again I think there is a great deal of injustice, inspired often by envy which it is irritating to contemplate against what is contemptuously termed *les gens du monde*, who besides having given us our most remarkable statesmen and rulers have also produced Catullus, Dante, Bacon, Montaigne, Ronsard, Sir Philip Sidney, Shelley, Pushkin, Tolstoi, Tourgeneff; their frivolity, their selfishness, their extravagance, etc. are always spoken of; their qualities are taken for granted, and the charm of their qualities is that they were matters of course to them themselves; things which they did naturally and thought no more of than of being decently clothed, and these qualities have a great attraction when they are tested in the crucible of tragic events – such as the French Revolution – and they produce the gold of heroism. Heroism too of, to me, a particularly attractive kind – 'the unselfishness of the selfish, the unworldliness of the worldly', suddenly manifest without fuss, cant or pretension. I like the account of Biron's death in the French Revolution,[2] I like the manifestation of that kernel of unflinching and uncompromising instinct which, blent with the utmost cynicism and irony, has caused men in various epochs to go laughingly to death for a cause or a creed in which they did not believe. Again I have personally noticed this, that [the] idle frivolous class regard the other with <u>respect</u> and accept their censure with indifference, whereas the laborious often regard the frivolous with outward contempt mingled with an inward gnawing and hankering envy. We know the frequent combination of the socialist and the snob. Do not misunderstand me or think I am either blind to what is hollow and sham in 'social' (hateful word) life or to what is great and noble in the lives of those who renounce it and all its works.

All I say is that tolerance is necessary on both sides, the frivolous have their qualities and the strenuous and sober have faults, which should suffice to prevent them from continually seeking for the motes in the eyes of others.

There is another point, of which you were possibly thinking. It is sometimes very irritating – to the strenuous – when the frivolous arrogate to themselves authority in a province which does not belong to them.

As Sarcey said about the *public des Mardis* at the Théâtre Français, *Ils viennent pour voir et se faire voir c'est bien; mais la pièce est que cela les regarde?*[3]

But here again do we not all ... prefer the favourable judgement of such people, if sincere, to that of the professional critics and *gens de métier?* ...

The critics ignored Shelley; the *gens du monde* discovered him. I know the reverse of the medal; you need not mention it. The intellectual snobberies, pretensions and ignorance, fashion, etc. I only say that it is <u>good that they should exist</u>; they have their function and it is not so narrow as is generally conceived.

Look at the judgement of the professional painters on Ruskin at the time of the Ruskin trial: the ignorant amateurs were wiser.[4]

Personally the opinion I most respect and most care for is that of *des honnêtes gens* who are neither specialists nor workers, who live away from cliques and coteries and have no other motive than the desire of expressing their likes and dislikes and if they are intelligent I think their criticism is the best which is to be got. ...

Yours affec., Maurice

1 Vernon Lee's *Ariadne in Mantua* (1903), a romance in five acts. In 1908 M.B wrote an essay on it, republished in *Punch and Judy* (1924).

2 Armand Louis de Gontaut, Duc de Lauzun and Duc de Biron, French general and politician, born 1747, guillotined 1793.
3 Francisque Sarcey (1828–99), French dramatic critic and novelist.
4 Whistler sued Ruskin for libel in 1877 after Ruskin had written of *The Falling Rocket* 'I never expected to hear of a coxcomb ask 200 guineas for flinging a pot of paint in the public's face.' He was only awarded nominal damages.

HENRY BREWSTER   [London]
                                                        21 Dec. 1903
My dear H. B.,

... I want to consult you about something. Whether or not it [is] profitable or sensible for me to go on writing plays.

A great many people tell me it is a mistake and nearly all are unanimous in urging me to write other things instead. What they say is this: 'If your plays could ever be acted, well and good, but if they are unactable, why not choose another form as, apart from the commercial and practical value of plays, which are a mere drug on the market, there is nothing which people are so little inclined to read and people who would read poems willingly stick at plays.'

Again I myself think that even if plays cannot be acted they should when read give the reader the impression that, given ideal actors, they could be acted; they ought to be dramatic enough for that, and if mine do not convey that impression, I am perhaps following a will of the wisp. But if one does write plays I am sure that the only way to reach any excellence is by constant practice and I think in my case that my latest work shows improvement on the earlier. ...

Again it is the form in which my thoughts naturally express themselves ...

                                                        Yours, M.B.

EDMUND GOSSE   Tatishow[1]
                                                        July 17, Sunday, 1904
My beloved Chermaître,

I am at headquarters and I start tomorrow for the further front to join the impetuous dragoon regiment to which I have been attached. I am enjoying myself wildly, sleeping in horseboxes and Chinese temples and travelling 6 miles in 24 hours in cramfull trains. China, this part of it, is a land of sand and rain and gold ... it is rich, green and incredibly fertile. I have learnt a little Chinese... The Chinese are like so many Brewsters *des hommes paîennes* if ever there were any. Resolutely certain that their mode of existence – to be content with very little and to take life as a flower and enjoying the evanescent fragrance of the hours but not to make the mistake of catching 'the strange disease of modern life'.[2] They know that rickshaws are more pleasant than motors. They are very aggravating all the same and their contempt, their victorious contempt, for the European and the way they make fools of us at every turn quietly and with a smile (Oh! I was so humiliated by every Chinese servant) is very exasperating. ... All is extremely interesting and thrilling here. I have got a white pony that gallops like mad and bites and kicks and heads and then suddenly becomes quite tame and sings a Chinese lullaby like a canary. I have yet another brown pony which snarls like a dog and hops like a flea. Tomorrow I shall be scouring the blue, blue hills of Manchuria, 'mysterious land surrounded by a lot of sand'. ... The Japs are quite close. If one has realised the Chinese, one can have nothing but contempt for the Japs and their German ways. They flood the world with imitation soda water and imitation Bryant and May matches which explode in one's pocket. I hope devoutly they will be beaten. I suppose I ought [not] to think that but I do, and that's an end on't. I think the Russians are behaving splendidly.

    God bless you my Dear,

Yours, M.

1 M.B. went to Manchuria as correspondent of the *Morning Post* for the Russo-Japanese war. He was attached to a cavalry brigade of the 1st Siberian Army Corps commanded by General Samsonoff and several times came under fire. He recorded his impressions of this period in *The Puppet Show of Memory*, *With the Russians in Manchuria* (1905), and *A Year in Russia* (1907).
2 Matthew Arnold, 'The Scholar-Gipsy'.

EDMUND GOSSE

3, Gray's Inn Place
High Holborn[1]
20th May, 1905

My dear Cherm,

    Have you seen Arthur's poems?[2] Some are as good as any he has written but he would have made the book better had he selected its contents in a more critical spirit. For instance he includes a Coronation Ode on the King, stuff one could reel out by the yard, if, as Dr. Johnson said, one abandoned one's mind to it. There is an Ode to Japan in which he pats them on the back (as if all these thousands of years they had only been dolls!) and he says in a stanza which made me rock with laughter

> From us you shall acquire
> Stern labour, sterner truth (1)
> . . . . .
> And that strong faith we reckon ours (2)

(1) a hint that they should be honest in business matters.

(2) a suggestion, I suppose, that they should become Church of England.

I have told him that to tell the Japanese they will acquire stern labour from us is as if he were to tell Cicero he would acquire the art of writing Latin Prose from a 4th form boy at Eton. Good gracious! Labour from us! The Japs of all people, who put the bees and the ants to shame by their unremitting sedulous patient toil and love of toil. And this advice coming from Eton, that citadel of sloth and silly toil. (I have made a verse; you see it would be a good beginning for a sonnet.)

> Oh! citadel of sloth and silly toil
> Where games are more important than all work,
> Where every boy's ambition is to shirk
> His duty and to hoodwink and to foil
> His stupid teachers.

The reason I am hinting this is that, as Arthur has now six books[3] in the press, I hope you will see that before they appear they pass through the sieve of your criticism because there are always unnecessary branches in his work which spoil the effect of the whole and could easily be removed. There are some beautiful things in his latest production. I have told him all this myself, but unostentatiously and without letting him know there is this conspiracy, do exercise a restraining hand, the hand of a kind gardener on his exuberantly flowering wilderness. What a pity he isn't Headmaster!

Yours, M.B.

1 He was staying with Eddie Marsh.

2 Arthur Benson, *Peace, and Other Poems* (1905).
3 Other books published in 1905: *Edward FitzGerald, The Thread of Gold, The Upton Letters* and, in 1906, *Walter Pater* and *The House of Quiet*.

VERNON LEE   British Embassy, St. Petersburg
                                                    August 4, 1905

My dear Miss Paget,

... I have just been reading an article of yours in the *Westminster* on a funeral in a Greek church.[1] It set me thinking. I don't believe the impression you got from the Greek church was entirely due to its being a Greek church but partly because it was a Greek church out of its proper place, in a Catholic country.

For I have got just that impression from Mass at the Roman Catholic Cathedral at Westminster where all the pomp of Rome is mingled with all the order and tidiness of England, so much so that I don't feel as if I was in a Catholic church. If you talk, a verger comes and tells you to be quiet, and the candles don't gutter; it is all swept and garnished. At Arundel at the R.C. church the effect is exactly the same. There is no tawdriness, no hurry, and the shadow of Protestantism is everywhere, because, I suppose, the form religion takes in a country depends on the national characteristics, and the characteristics of England are staid and Protestant.

Now the impression one receives from the Greek church in a Russian village or in the Cathedral of the Assumption at Moscow is totally different from what you describe as happening at Venice. At Moscow one is struck by the extraordinary mixture of devoutness and practicalness, a kind of *lares et penates* pagan quality in the worship, utterly devoid of self-consciousness, and being performed in the manner in which these things must be done because they have always been done like that.

The church is crowded to begin with, every class, peasants, children, women, soldiers, generals, officials, all standing up in a crowd and every single person carrying on his particular devotions separately. For instance one man remains stolidly immovable when certain saints are mentioned but prostrates himself at the name of others; he invokes his particular favourite saint more than others.

Then sometimes quite suddenly a peasant will give way to an access of devotion and prostrate himself nine times running. All the time the magnificent bass singing is going on.

You ought to go to Moscow and write about it; and do go to the Cathedral at Westminster on Sunday and see if you share my impression.

Yours, Maurice

1 'The Bread-Threader's Funeral and the Church of the Greeks', *Westminster Gazette*, 1 August.

EDMUND GOSSE   Foreign O.
                                                September 5th, 1905

Text for September 5.
'Remember the almond tree in the days of thy holiday.'
Epistles. N.48.49[1]

Mon Cher,
            I am a faded almond tree
              On which there is no flower,
            Leafless & bare, O Misery,
            I am a faded almond tree;
            In vain the sun shall shine on me,
              In vain shall fall a shower,
            I am a faded almond tree
              On which there is no flower.

London is hot and rainy and empty. The Foreign Office is stuffy and full of papers and desks and scrapers and messengers and boxes and other inutilities.

            I would I were in France,
            There where the Gosses are,
            From morn to noon we'd dance,
            Under the deodar,
            From noon to eve we'd rest
            Under the palimpsest,
            From eve to dawn we'd sing a glee
            Under the branch of the almond tree!

Au revoir, I must stop. Je vous prie de saluer Mrs. Gosse de ma part.

Votre, M.

1 Cf. Ecclesiastes XII, 1 and 5.

[61]

VERNON LEE   British Embassy, St. Petersburg
                                                         Jan. 7, 1906

My dear Vernon (Allow me this familiarity),

Although I never hear from you, every now and then I hear of what you have thought about. ...Yesterday in the English bookshop I saw a new book of yours and bought *The Spirit of Rome*.¹ I don't know if it's good or bad and don't care. I only know that in a curious way it brought back to me all sorts of past days and that when I read about the river god I thought about our walk in the early spring when the spring was like the spring in a lyric or on a Chinese white milky vase ... and I felt I wanted to write to you.²...

Often in reading articles by you I have come across a sentence which I particularly felt and understood, not that any one of your sentences were meant for me, but it is all the better when they are not 'meant' and yet find the exact response. ...

I should like to read what you would write about [Moscow] as a place. It has no beauty really, nothing which we enjoy anywhere else, no art, nothing stimulating either in the place or the people and yet I find it has for me an extraordinary charm. It is dirty, shabby, rather sordid, very untidy, backward, ignorant, vulgar in some parts and ostentatious – and yet – it's the people, I suppose, and I suppose their charm arises from their good nature and simplicity. One can't help loving a cabman who says to you, 'I don't know what I would have done if God hadn't sent you to me last night when you drove home. I told all my friends that everybody had gone home and there was no one to drive, but God sent me a Barin, and such a Barin who paid double the fare.'³ 'I suppose you said God sent you a fool,' I said. 'O Barin,' he answered, 'don't offend God.'

Write to me.

                                        Yours, M.B. (Maurice)

1 Published 1906.
2 Cf. *The Puppet Show of Memory*. In the chapter 'Stimulants' in *Lost Lectures* M.B. wrote: 'Sight-seeing with Vernon Lee was sight-seeing indeed. It was the opposite of scampering through a gallery with Baedeker, and ticking off what had been "done". It was there for ever in the haunted, many-corridored and echoing palace of her imagination, and, after you had seen such things with her, in yours as well.'
3 In *A Year in Russia* (1907), p. 295, M.B. wrote: 'Barin, I suppose everybody knows, means a *monsieur*, in contradistinction to the lower class.'

British Embassy, St. Petersburg
                                              Jan. 31, 1906

My dear Vernon,

I got your letter yesterday and I cannot tell you what an immense pleasure it was to hear from you;[1] I am all right and I came here to see the Benckendorffs who are here. I have finished *The Spirit of Rome*. It took me back into past days. Rome is a place – like Algiers to you – which I enjoyed afterwards; while I was there I was unhappy and long-ing to go. This was partly because I loathed the Diplomatic Service which is a really degrading profession I think. Of course I know that this is nonsense and that *il n'y a pas de son métier;* but if one finds one is tied to a thing one doesn't like, the sooner one cuts oneself away from it the better. That is just what Americans never hesitate or fear to do. ...

Have you read *L'Idiot* by Dostoievsky? I think it is the most aston-ishing book I have ever read in my life. Not D's best book, perhaps in some ways his worst, and yet his best all the same in that all his qualities and faults are in it at their intensest and the qualities are the result of the faults and vice versa. It is constructed or rather not constructed without a trace of skill; the setting is most of the time wildly impossible and most of the characters unlike anyone in the world and absurdly fantastically impossible and yet profoundly true and as living as Ethel Smyth and Maria Pasolini are living.[2] There is more love and pity in the book than in any I have ever read except the Gospel of St. Mark, and some portions of it seem to me sublime. When I say the characters are impossible I do not mean they are like Meredith's creatures, of another planet; they are impossible mainly because they don't happen to exist but they are human and alive with the humanity and life of this planet. ...

I also want to know if you have read Chesterton's[3] books, *Napoleon of Notting Hill, Heretics*? I like his <u>ideas</u>.

                                              Yours, M.B.

1 Letter dated 25 January, part of which is reproduced in Smyth, p. 206.
2 Count and Countess Pasolini were great friends both of M.B. and of Vernon Lee. They lived in the Palazzo Sciarra, and the Count was the original of 'Count Sciarra' in M.B.'s story 'The Luncheon Party' in *Half a Minute's Silence and Other Stories*. See *The Puppet Show of Memory*.
3 Gilbert Keith Chesterton (1874–1936) was to become a close friend. He, M.B. and Hilaire Belloc came to be regarded as a triumvirate of Roman Catholic writ-ers and their triple portrait *Conversation Piece* by James Gunn hangs in the National Portrait Gallery.

L. C.   British Embassy, St. Petersburg
                                                      Feb. 16, 06

My dear L. C.,

... Do you know that you and Ethel Smyth are the only two people I now correspond with in the world – I mean I correspond uninterruptedly, write to and receive letters from in spite of time and space. ...

The Bencks. are staying with her sister, Countess Bobrinsky, a delightful house, with people pouring in and out of it as they like, a gramophone going on all day long, a huge lame dog, a small fluffy Chinese dog. Two daughters, one married, quite young, 19, and exactly like a rose – an ordinary rose. The other unmarried, also quite young and like a flower that grows on the Alps where I have never been. Two boys, one 18 and like a very nice fox-terrier and one 12 – a mischievous boy ... with a soft pudding face and sparkling grey eyes. He writes poetry and has for the last 6 years, in fact ever since he could write, and has also printed a book. It is most amazing, extraordinary ideas for a boy and some of the poems much better than any modern Russian poetry I have seen, and it goes on and on, lyrics, ballads, plays. He is now writing a tragedy which happens in ancient Rome, under Corneille and Racine influence. At the same time he is not the least priggish but an ordinary, very mischievous and romping boy, brimful of fun: he amazes me. He printed and published his book two years ago and sold it for the Red Cross. The other boy (18 years) is a budding engineer absorbed in electricity and politics... The whole family is extraordinarily like a sort of *Guerre et la Paix* household ...

Goodbye,

                                                      Yrs. M.B.

L. C.   [British Embassy, St Petersburg]
                                                  Friday, March 2, 06

My dear L. C.,

... I am sitting in a small wooden room with big wooden beams on the ceiling, a deal dado, books, a writing table, a big divan, very white and clean ... Conny and Pierre Benckendorff are playing mandolines, Natalie is pouring out tea in a cerulean frock and another friend, a boy of 17, is playing the guitar. They are playing the Russian song you copied out. It is the first day of spring here. Dazzling cold air, huge patches of hard snow everywhere and thick gulfs of black mud where there is no snow.

The meeting of the boys and their two old Russian nurses in white caps was very touching... The nurses have been thanking God without a second's pause all day. I am very happy here and infinitely sad at the same time. ... Mandoline sounds suddenly becoming rather delicious (out of chaos; hitherto chaos predominant and quarrel about who is wrong and out of tune when everyone is). Sisters and brothers seem to me facsimile, the same all over the world. So much so that when they either laugh to dying point or quarrel over any particular thing I see almost tangible ghosts of childhood.

... Cabman's account yesterday of big robbery at bank in Moscow and revolutionaries with bombs one of the most delicious things I ever heard. Asked him if the robbers were to be sympathized with. He said 'Of course.' Asked him if he would have liked the money, £800,000. No. Much too much, he said – the sort of sum which would do for you (for me, M.B.) because if you had it you would be able to pay me double my fare and I should be able to thank you.

M.B.

VERNON LEE   British Embassy, St. Petersburg
                                                        March 3, 1906

My dear Vernon,

Since we are now once more *en relation* I am going to dun you! At least I advance a claim for a long-standing debt. I have been reading *Juvenilia*[1] and it is that which brought it back to my mind. You remember – I know you remember – my telling you of how when I was 7 or 8 years old I was promised a prize if during three days I obtained 20 counters for doing twenty things well on 20 different occasions, be it Latin, French, music, arithmetic or drawing, how I got the 20 counters and bought for my prize The *Prince of the 100 Soups*,[2] how I revelled in it, dramatized it, had it specially bound with little soup-tureens on the back, read it until I knew it almost by heart. Never had I so revelled in a book, which seemed to be at last the incarnation of what I had always hoped a book might someday prove to be, and then when I next got a prize how I went to buy another book by the same author, hoping for a similar experience, and the book, you remember, was *Belcaro*![3]

Belcaro, which I have never read till this day because every time I approach it I am seized by the same passion of disappointment which I felt on that occasion. Well, I feel for this enormous injustice, this unutterable wrong, you owe me a reparation and there is only one reparation you can make and that is to write me another story, the story which I thought *Belcaro* was going to be. ...

Providence has arranged for the possibility of the compensation by the fact that I shall enjoy the story as much now as I would have done then and perhaps more. Therefore, Vernon, I want another story, another puppet show in narrative or a fairy tale or a ghost story or merely a story, but it must happen in Italy. In Italy of the XVIIIth century or if you like any other century, except the present.

Only it must be serious, I mean not a burlesque, not more than the *100 Soups* was, and I never as a child quite approved of the *Horseless Cavalry* in which I suspected that you were not taking your story quite as seriously as you ought to be doing. That is the debt you owe me, the debt which I have long meant to claim. ...

Yours ever, Maurice

1 *Juvenilia: Being a Second Series of Essays on Sundry Aesthetical Questions*, 2 vols. (1887).
2 *The Prince of the 100 Soups: A Puppet-Show in Narrative*, edited and with an introduction by Vernon Lee, 'Author of *Belcaro*, etc' (1883).
3 *Belcaro: Being Essays on Sundry Aesthetical Questions* (1883). 'In 1927 she performed an act of contrition, when she brought out *For Maurice: five unlikely stories*': Peter Gunn, *Vernon Lee*, p. 87.

HILAIRE BELLOC   British Embassy, St. Petersburg
March 3rd, 1906

My dear Hilaire,

Thanks by the million and congratulations on your speech.[1] ... Well, it's a great thing that there should be someone in the House of Commons and elsewhere who dares say exactly what he thinks. ...The attitude of the Government seems to me unsatisfactory from every point of view. ... All impartial people who come from South Africa say it's all rot; that Chinese labour is (1) necessary (2) not slavery or any of the things it's accused of being.

Now I am sorry when a question of fact like this becomes a party question and it's a peculiar gift of the Liberal party to adopt this sort of question and deluge the world with cant about it. ... I am not a Liberal, never was but I am a <u>radical</u>: I am a Tory when it is possible but I am in favour of the radical change of what I believe to be wrong.[2]

Now as to your salary. Go to *M.P.*, get hold of Ware.[3] ... Say you are willing to write exclusively for *M.P.* ... on condition of regular salary ... Now as you supply them with the best prose they get and prose which is not only good but universally appreciated I think the argument would have weight. ... I did the same with *M.P.* I refused to write except for monthly pay and I succeeded in getting them to agree. ... If they won't [agree] threaten this: that you, Marsh, I, Raymond Asquith,[4] Bron,[5] Chesterton and a conservative – mention a conservative – and any friends you like to mention will start a paper of our own in which, assisted by Donald Tovey on music, Arthur Benson on education, Vernon Lee on Italy and art, Edmund Gosse, Chesterton, Arthur Symons[6] on literature, numerous Russians on Russia through me, and all our numerous friends will combine and that it will be to their disadvantage. I am sure that with a little bullying Ware will eventually cave in. At the same time say the following prayer: 'Lord, remember David the King and all his grace', and burn a candle to St. Michael, St. Luke the patron saint of literature and St. Peter (who cannot refuse a request). And pray also to the Mother of God to intercede for you on this <u>particular point</u>. Say you want a fixed salary from *Morning Post*, not money vaguely.

Yours with blessings, Maurice

1 Belloc had been elected Liberal M.P. for South Salford and had made his maiden speech on 27 February attacking the Liberal government for its policy on the deportation of Chinese labourers from the South African mines. Belloc had written to M.B. on that day describing his speech. Part of the letter is reproduced in Robert Speaight's *Hilaire Belloc*, pp. 210-11.

2 In a previous letter to Belloc he had written: 'I become more and more radical every day: but I have no special belief in the Liberal party: i.e. I do not believe in its radical difference to the Conservative party...what is more conservative than free trade?'

3 M.B. had been trying to persuade *The Morning Post* to give Belloc a permanent job. On 20 September he was appointed literary editor but resigned in 1910 following disagreements with the editor. See Speaight, pp. 218, 257–9. Fabian Arthur Goulstone Ware (1869–1949), educationist and soldier, was editor 1905–11. Major-general 1918, K.C.V.O. 1922.

4 (1878–1916), a man of outstanding academic distinction and promise, son of H. H. Asquith. Practised as a barrister and was appointed junior counsel to the Inland Revenue 1914, which would normally have led to a judgeship, but was killed while serving in the Grenadier Guards. Was at Oxford with M.B. and Belloc and was a close friend.

5 Auberon Thomas Herbert (1876–1916), succeeded as 8th Baron Lucas and Dingwall, 1905. As a Liberal politician held government office 1908–15 (P.C. 1912) but despite his position as a member of the government and the fact that he had lost a leg as a result of wounds received when acting as the *Times* correspondent in the South African War, joined the Royal Flying Corps as a pilot and was killed. In his honour M.B. wrote *In Memoriam A. H.*(1917), which first appeared in the *New Statesman*. Met M.B. at Oxford and remained a close friend.

6 (1865–1945), poet and critic.

L. C.   British Embassy, St. Petersburg
                 March 6, 1906

Dear L. C.,

… I spent a week at the Doctor's… Extraordinary how many people can live in so small a space. Doctor, wife, three children, mother-in-law, governess and two servants. I slept in sitting room and the odd thing is that it wasn't dirty and I don't think they would like a bigger house if one offered them one.

Doctor very nice, wife charming, said to me he had never told them a word about the war and they were longing to know if he had been hungry ever. Children delicious. Doctor frightfully depressed by having had, I think, illusions in Mongolia about new Golden Age coming about and then finding nothing of the sort. He can't read the newspapers from disgust.

I sat whole of one morning in the hospital, seeing peasants come, tell illnesses, be bandaged and given medicine. … Doctor said most of their diseases came from stuff which they were given by friends; they love medicine and take it all at once when given any. …

The fact is that things have never been so bad in Russia as they are now. Never has there been so much chaos and such awful things happening. In a way the worse it is the better, because it will make the catastrophe all the more thorough and the sweeping away… I am convinced this will come and that it will be all swept away. …

             Yours, M.B.

VERNON LEE Sosnofka, Tambov
March 30, 1906

This is the second time in my life, my dear Vernon, I am writing to you from this writing table in a room panelled with fresh, unpainted, unpolished oak, a white-washed ceiling with big beams in it, a small room, smaller than the sitting-rooms in the Palmerino. Count Benckendorff and his sister are playing Vingt with the village schoolmaster and his wife; a young boy, Tino Lobanoff, is twanging the violin and I am writing to you. On the table lies your *Genius Loci* and on the sofa lies *Hauntings*[1] and it is perhaps the act of having been *feuillétting Genius Loci* for the last ten minutes that put it into my head to write to you. ... I wondered how this country will strike you, this country where there is no past in the sense there is a past in Italy, France, England or Germany. But God is I think a versatile creator and knows what he is about. He knew in making Russia and America that something else was needed. *Une nouvelle chorde à la lyre*. I have been wondering whether you would have the feeling here you had in the Alps, that you were cut off from the world. I think not; ... it is all so poignantly human here. One has the same feeling as one had in Ireland and one understands when one looks at the brown soaking plains, the mud, the straw, the dirt, the untidiness, the endless plain with its cleft hollows, monotonous villages, churches (pink, white and green modern Byzantine), the windmills, the long procession of peasants in dirty sheepskin with beards, sitting sideways on a long cart or a sledge, that though it may be impossible to state in plain terms the attraction of the country, it is one which a native would sigh for in exile.

I had been here only in summer and autumn before and now I have witnessed the prelude to spring. Not Wordsworth's first fine day in March ... everything is so much later here, but the prelude of spring, the tuning up before the overture, the melting of the snow, the 'floods of spring'. The snow begins to melt and the plain instead of being a huge white expanse of shining immaculateness becomes a patched thing, stretches of dazzling white and then patches of brown earth and patches of green, and patches of brown with green in it (corn), and then stretches of half-melted snow, steely and reflecting the blue sky and in the distance soft outlines of brown trees and over all the larks singing. Then above the water is a wonderful sight, brown woods reflected into still white and grey limpidity and trees rising like ghosts out of the water, brown, delicate and frail.

[69]

There is plenty of human past here, at least the human past is the same as the human present. It is one long monotonous succession even as the landscape, but there is, properly speaking, no historical past. Would you mind that? I think not, for a change.

Thank you, Vernon, for republishing *Hauntings*. I have written my joy in the *Morning Post*. I couldn't keep it to myself and wanted others to share it. In all Europe there are grateful people. ...

Yours, M.B.

1 *Hauntings. Fantastic Stories*, 1892.

VERNON LEE   British Embassy, St. Petersburg
August 2, 1906

My dear Vernon,

Thank you very much for your letter. I am sorry you didn't go to see Countess B[enckendorff]. I wouldn't have asked you to if it had meant the disagreeable things you foresaw. Empty reception-rooms, footmen, etc. If you went or go in the morning, you would simply be shown up by a small German servant into a little sitting room full of books and photographs which might be a part of the Palmerino. Happily some people stamp themselves on the most ungrateful surroundings and the personality of Cts. B. makes the conventional Embassy surroundings an <u>impossibility</u>. She blots it out; so that there are no empty reception rooms, no smiling footmen, no smart people, but instead you might find Maggie Ponsonby or Lady Constance, or Ethel. What surprises me is that you shouldn't have guessed this. Surely if someone said to you 'I can't go and see Countess Pasolini because I can't face the Roman Palace, the Italian ceremony, the Swiss guard in the front hall and the private priest in the background', you would laugh very much! Well, the <u>case is exactly parallel</u>. Just as Maria would conquer or get the better <u>of any such surroundings,</u> so does Cts. B. However, there is no reason why you should have guessed this except from the fact of her having friends like Maggie, Ethel and me and also from the fact of Russians being far more simple in themselves and their lives even than the Italians, which is saying a good deal. However some day you shall meet in my house. ...

Bless you Vernon for all your kindness to me and goodbye.

Yours, Maurice

VERNON LEE   [St Petersburg]
                                                    Oct. 10, 1906

My dear Vernon,

... I was interested in what you say about Bayreuth. I agree
absolutely. So far as Bayreuth itself goes, the only enjoyment to me is
the orchestra, which when I heard it I thought divine and better than
any other I had heard. Now I daresay you hear just as good at Munich
and elsewhere. Then you didn't. As to Wagner ... yes, D'Annunzio has
the same, exactly the same quality of slowness and hypnotic
mesmerism, also (I think) the gift of doing something to language which
introduces another element in it, just as Wagner does with sound. At its
worst it is like the noise people make by rubbing the rim of a glass of
water, at its best it is something very mysteriously beautiful, and then
attack it as one does and may, the fact of the genius and the bigness of
scale remains, and the peculiar things Wagner has said which no one
else has. For instance, the 'sharpness of death' that is in the *traurige
Weise* of Kurneval's tune on the pipe in the last act of Tristan, the infinite sadness of Brunhilde's appeal to Sigismund in *Valküre* Act II and
the joyousness of Siegfried's horn-call. What I like best of all is the
Meistersinger; as for *Parsifal* I abhor it. It is a grotesque parody of the
Mass with conjuring tricks and oh! the length. Another artist who
seems to me in this category is Swinburne. Almost every poem of Swinburne is too long, not because it is too long in actual size and length but
because everything that is said lasts too long, the tempo is too much
drawn out. Take one of his finest poems, the 'Elegy on Baudelaire'. It
misses being quite magnificent because every stanza is too long,
whereas the whole poem might have been twice as long and yet not too
long if Catullus had written it for instance. That is why I think Racine
(you will disagree) is such a great poet; he is as perfect a master over his
means as Mozart and gives you a thousand lights and shades. ...

                                                    Yours, Maurice

HILAIRE BELLOC   St. Petersburg
                                                    Nov. 9, 06

My dear H.,

... Do you really think my sonnets are good? I wonder. I was fear-
fully snubbed the other day for publishing a book of verse at all by a

                            [71]

high English official; he said it was ridiculous. He hadn't read it and didn't mean to, but he said this before 25 people after dinner and they all laughed and I felt a bloody fool. In France nobody thinks it odd if you write verse, or here either. They talk about it naturally, and in England it was so until the reign of Charles II and even later, until 1815 I suppose, and then the damned Puritans cast their stinking tarpaulin of respectability over their filthy vices and pretended to be virtuous. They will surely be damned. Bless you Hilaire and thank you for your Sonnet which has more strength and dignity than anything I ever wrote.

Yours, M.B.

EDWARD MARSH [Russia]

March 18, 1907

My dear E.,

You wish to know the truth of the mad dog incident. You shall. It was like this. Countess Bobrinsky's[1] small white Chinese dog was violated by an enormous mastiff and had two puppies. The puppies were huge. And when, after confinement, the white tiny Chinese dog began to show signs of malaise, nobody thought it odd, because it seemed natural that a small Chow should show signs of malaise after so shattering an experience. It was the opposite of the adage. A mouse gave birth to a mountain and nobody was surprised at the mouse seeming not quite the thing after the experience. On the third day the Chow, whose name was Folly, began to lick everybody feverishly and to run about the house. It complained also of seeing imaginary snakes and *Weltschmerz* generally. On the fourth day it licked an open sore on my hand and snapped at my nose too and succeeded in biting my nose twice without drawing blood. On the fifth day it bit the maid, the other dog, its husband, and the housekeeper; but all this biting was said to be in self-defence, since the big dog had looked at the puppies and the little dog had then spat at it, flown at it and finally bitten it, and the maid and the housekeeper had been bitten in the separating of them. On the sixth day the Chow died. Its last words were 'Roll up the map of China', but some authorities aver it said 'More bones.' Then a post-mortem examination was held and its brain was put under the microscope. In its brain, which was blue, a small red spot, bright as a ruby, was discernible. The doctors said the dog must have been mad and the

Countess Bobrinsky, the maid, the housekeeper, son and daughter, were sent to the Pasteur Institute and inoculated with mad Welsh rabbit, but not, as some people now say, with March hare. It appears, according to the latest authorities, that hares are seldom mad and never in March.

Two live rabbits were inoculated with portions of the dead Folly. Our inoculation proceeded day by day and my body turned blue and my hair fell, dwindled and lessened and grew slowly by degrees gradually less, and soft as sleeping summer, silken down. Countess Bobrinsky had heart-beatings and gasped for breath and [had] an intermittent headache. The housekeeper had nettle rash and spasms. The boy wrote an epic on inoculation and the gastric juices. The girl Countess, Sofie Bobrinsky, made feverish love to three doctors and the other dog sang like a canary. The rabbits went mad and died, like Charles II and Petronius Arbiter, civil to the last, with cynical dignity. In the meantime the news came from Xarkoff that a man whose ear had been bitten by a dog which subsequently had gone mad, had also died of hydrophobia.

After being inoculated twelve times and when our bodies were like that of St. Sebastian and permanently disfigured and our whole systems had been convulsed, as though by earthquake and eclipse, the treatment ceased. The big dog is still sane (it was also inoculated) but the two puppies died with eyes full of perished dreams and wrecks of forgotten delusions. The reason of this fact was ... because Folly had licked her puppies, not bitten them, but merely licked them as a mother should. ...

Yours ever, M.B.

1 M.B. stayed with the Bobrinskys at Smielo (*The Puppet Show of Memory*). This letter was published in Marsh's *A Number of People*.

L.C.   c/o British Embassy, St. Petersburg
                                                        13 Oct. 07

My dear L.C.,

I write you a line to say that I have come back to St. P. ... I stayed in a most amusing place at Kharkov ... The people I stayed with at Kharkov are newish friends of mine, Prince [Mirsky] and his wife. He is a charming witty oldish man. ... She was a Bobrinsky, rather silent, country-loving, town-hating, independent, photographing, south-windy ocean kind, seeing everything – transparent blue eyed, steel-true, gentle. ...

[73]

(It's an awful thing. They've got an English governess who takes in *Morning Post* and they read all my articles which makes it very difficult for me to write anything now. Luckily she, Princess Mirsky, told me she had never seen peasants' religion explained so well in print before and that it was exactly what she had always seen. This was most comforting.)

Four children. Boy, 17, black-haired, clever as possible.[1] Girl about 19, a little deformed, very nice and intelligent, very pessimistic about herself, very sensible and self-depreciatory. Small boy at military school. Small girl with a plait. They live at Kharkov in the country in an untidy Trianon house full of people, about 30 visitors, neighbours etc. coming and going. No dressing for dinner and dinner at 1 and supper at 9. Delicious and lovely park. They are now at Petersburg. ...

Goodbye, M.

1 D. S. Mirsky (1890–1939). After serving in the Russian Army he escaped to England where M.B. arranged financial support (Letley, p. 194). He was a writer and author of *The Intelligentsia of Great Britain*. He became a communist and was persuaded to return to Russia where he died in a prison hospital. He dedicated his *Contemporary Russian Literature 1881–1925* (1925) to M.B. whom he acknowledges as an authority on Russia. See G. S. Smith, *D. S. Mirsky. A Russian-English Life* (2000); Nina Lavroukine, article *Chesterton Review*, 1988, vol. XIX, no. 1.

VERNON LEE   3, Gray's Inn Place, High Holborn, W.C.
                                                      Jan. 10th, 1908

Dear Vernon,
    ... I have been reading *The Sentimental Traveller*.[1] Apart from the beauty of these papers I was struck by the charm of the glimpses of biography. ...

Ethel is in England... Opera negotiations are going on at Vienna and from time to time the music she composed to some French poems by Henri de Régnier[2] with accompaniment for flute, harp, triangle and a few strings is produced at concerts, both public and private. I heard two of them last summer; I thought them exquisite. The quintessence of Ethel – delicate, strange, and potent in rhythm, delicious as to sound. Out of the strong has come sweetness with a vengeance.

What you say about the small effect produced upon her contemporaries is not, I think, surprising. Apart from the fact that the educated musical public in England is small, Ethel's music, at least the music of her operas, is as a German critic, to my mind, rightly explained, so <u>individual</u> as to be almost disagreeable. A man in Prague (in fact the critic to whom I have just alluded) wrote an extremely interesting article about her *Wreckers*.³ He said that the first time he heard the opera he hated it. He went the first night ... When the performance was over he went home meaning to slate it. Then as he sat down to write, he said to himself: 'Is it true that this music is so bad, or is it possibly my fault? Have I perhaps failed to understand it?' He waited. He went back the second night and came back convinced that what he had heard was magnificent. Then he explained that he considered the reason of this to lie in the intensely individual quality of the music. He felt there was something bleak, tempestuous and uncompromising about it, a kind of quality you find in Ibsen's poetical dramatic work or in Rodin's sculpture, something which does not meet you halfway, something which does not hold out soft arms to embrace you but conquers you with the sword. I think this is rather true. I have heard *The Wreckers* in Prague; it was badly done, the orchestra played vilely, but it struck me as a magnificent production, but then I knew the music rather well. I have heard her play and sing it several times.

As regards you, I think you have made a great impression on your contemporaries, certainly on Europe if not on England, and then, after all, there are a great many people to whom you would not wish to appeal.

Please write to me again soon.

Yours affectionately, Maurice

1 *The Sentimental Traveller: Notes on Places* had recently been published. M.B.'s article on this book was printed in *The Morning Post* on 20 January 1908 and reprinted in *Punch and Judy*.

2 Henri François Joseph de Régnier (1864–1936), French poet and novelist. In 1907 Ethel Smyth had composed settings for three of his poems: *Odelette*, *La Danse* and *Chrysilla*.

3 Opera by Ethyl Smyth to a libretto by Henry Brewster. After one performance at Leipzig it was produced at Prague in 1906 and M.B. came all the way from St Petersburg for the first night. See Ethel Smyth, *Maurice Baring*, p. 47; Christopher St John, *Ethel Smyth* pp. 105–10. Staged at His Majesty's Theatre in 1909 and Covent Garden in 1910.

H. G. WELLS   Sosnofka, Tambov
                                                    Nov. 3, 09
My dear H. G.,

I am miserable because I've finished *Ann Veronica*. Please write another at once.

I love it. I mean <u>amo</u>. Hunc librum amo. J'aime ce livre d'amour. Ich liebe dieses Buch leidenschaftlich. Amo questo libro con amore.

I am in love with Ann Veronica. You know why I like your books so much. It's because they are bursting with love for the people they describe.

Even if you describe something you hate you understand it and the hate goes. You have exactly the same quality Dostoievsky has got. An infinite capacity for loving and understanding all human things, not in theory but in practice.

More, more, more please.

                                                    M.B.

EDMUND GOSSE   6, North Street, Westminster
                                              16th March, 1910
My dear G.,

... As to handwriting, I am afraid I am incurable. A nurse began the reform movement in the later '70s; she gave it up in 1880. Then an English governess threw herself into the breach with all the enthusiasm and experience of middle age; she, however, gave it up towards 1883. In 1884 four schoolmasters resolved to deal with the question but they soon lost their illusions and their spirit was broken. In 1886 until 1891 it was a fitful dream of successive Eton masters but they one and all despaired. However, this beautiful and accurate machine is the remedy and the consolation.

                                               Yours always, M.B.

H. G. WELLS   Gagarinskaya [St Petersburg], 5
                                              29 January, 1911
My dear H.G.,

I am reading *The New Machiavelli* and in the next room someone is playing Beethoven on a pianoforte by means of a pianola. Rack my brains as I will, I can't remember if you like Beethoven. I don't mean whether you are 'musical' or not. I am not at all sure whether Beethoven is musical if it comes to that ... but that's not the point – the point is that whatever the nature of Beethoven's medium may [be] there is no doubt of the immense size of the man and the extraordinary wild adventures of his soul.

Reading your book – or reading anything by any man who thinks – makes me think all these things, books, symphonies, statues, pictures, poems, are like large question marks to the universe. Beethoven's most triumphant strains seem to me to have the question worked through them. I am scrawling these lines not because I have anything to say but because I have a fit of longing for London, my friends, and for you, H.G.

Yours, M.B.

LADY ISLINGTON   6, North Street, Westminster
                                              May 11th, 1911

Darling Anne,

... The event last week was Nathalie's wedding to Jasper Ridley.[1] He is so nice, you would like him very much. They were married at the Russian Church. It is a square room upstairs in Welbeck Street with a gold and painted screen shutting off the altar but open. In the middle of the church a small altar is placed ... Nathalie and Jasper stood in front of this and the priest [who was] in stiff gold vestments. Nathalie had a lovely gown made in very simple silvery white satin. She looked like an Italian picture, very dignified. They each held a taper with orange-blossom round it and at a given moment a strip of pink satin is put on the floor and they step on to it to show that they will be on the same strip of the world and not separated. There is a superstition that whoever steps on to it first will have the upper hand ... Nathalie took good care to step on to it first. Then two crowns have to be held over their heads, crowns like in a fairy tale, and the best men (she had three) hold them, and when one gets tired the others relieve him. The crown is very heavy and one had to hold it up with one hand. I was one of Jasper's best men. Then they drink three times out of the same cup and peck each other once, and at the end they walk three times round the altar with the crowns held over their head. It was very impressive. ... Directly the wedding was over they were married again at St. Margaret's, Westminster.

[77]

Evan[2] and I went to hear Ramsay MacDonald[3] and Belloc debate on Socialism, Belloc against. He made the most brilliant speech I ever heard, quite unprepared and without a note. He never hesitated once ....

Yours, Maurbags

1 Nathalie Benckendorff (d. 1968), d. Count Benckendorff. Married 28 April 1911 Jasper Nicholas Ridley (1887–1951), banker, 2nd son of 1st Viscount Ridley. K.C.V.O. 1946. The Ridleys were close friends of M.B. and named their eldest son (b. 1913) Jasper Alexander Maurice.
2 The Hon. Evan Charteris (1864–1930), son of the 10th Earl of Wemyss, practised at the parliamentary bar. K.C. 1919, Kt. 1932. Art lover and author (books included *Life and Letters of Sir Edmund Gosse*). In 1930 he married M.B.'s niece Lady Dorothy Browne, daughter of the 5th Earl of Kenmare and widow of Lord Edward Grosvenor. M.B. had dedicated *Russian Essays and Stories* (1908) to him.
3 James Ramsay MacDonald (1866–1940) Labour M.P. Leader of the Labour Party 1911, P.C. 1924, prime minister 1924 and 1929–35. The debate was before the South-West London Federation of the Independent Labour Party and the speeches were later published verbatim in a pamphlet *Socialism and the Servile State* with a foreword by Herbert Morrison.

H. G. WELLS   The Old Lodge, Magdalene College, Cambridge[1]

August 23, 1911

My dear H. G.,

I write to thank you for the charming days I spent in your house ...

When we got to Rouen the booking office clerk and the man at the Bureau de Renseignements were blackly pessimistic about the Southampton route. They said it was impossible to book further than Southampton ... At the last moment I settled to go by Dieppe... I went 3rd... The train was full of Music-Hall *artistes*, Italians, Greeks, jockeys, phonograph-sellers and a man who said he was a musical publisher and a chauffeur. There was also an American (a Socialist) who was the biggest liar I have ever seen. He said he knew all languages but his favourite language for conversation was Sanskrit. For the benefit of the company he wrote the Greek for man on a piece of paper. Then I asked him to write the Russian for man, as he said he knew Russian. With a fine gesture he made some marks on the piece of paper and said 'That is the Russian for a man.' I felt it almost must be. ...

Yours, Maurice Baring

1 M.B. was staying with Arthur Christopher Benson (1862–1925). Author and scholar. Educated at Eton and King's College, Cambridge, he had been a housemaster at Eton when M.B. was at school there but left in 1903 to become a fellow of Magdalene College, Cambridge, of which he became Master in 1915. Author of 'Land of Hope and Glory'.

EDMUND GOSSE

Sosnofka

Oct. 23, 1911

Cher Maître,

The book on Denmark[1] has not reached me but I stole a copy before leaving London and I read it last night in bed. I said I will read one chapter before going to bed. I read one and then another and then a third. I said I will read just a little more and I did and then I looked at my watch and saw it was two o'clock.

It is an exquisite and enchanting book. I laughed out loud again and again. It is delicious. All the more to me who have been in Denmark … It is most tantalising and leaves one longing for more.

You simply must write a volume on your first years in London among the Pre-Raphaelites, with vignettes of Rossetti, Swinburne, Marzials,[2] Morris – nobody can do this as you do it. It is so lucid, so fresh, and so perfect in its form, so satisfying to the slovenly journalist which I am… You can't think how I laughed last night. I am sleepy today from the vigil. More, more and more please…

I have no news to tell you except that a sprained ankle of mine which had been worrying me for a month has been cured in an unconventional manner. A peasant here who looks after or is supposed to look after the garden walks noticed I was lame and said he would cure my sprain at once if I would take off my stocking. I did, then he brought a large bunch of sting-nettles and soaked them in hot water and proposed that I should bind and rub the place with them.

I said: 'Do you want to sting me on purpose?' He said 'Yes.' I, after some slight hesitation, consented and lo and behold the sprain has gone. I am cured, tho' stung. I wondered afterwards whether wasps or bees would be equally efficacious. Perhaps Philip knows.[3]

Sting-nettles, said the man, cured any bruise and are especially good if you fell off a high ladder. Next time that happens to you in the House of Lords you will know what to do. But I am afraid there are

[79]

no sting-nettles in the House of Lords garden or in St. James's Park. But you might get the Lords to plant some.

Today is Sarah Bernhardt's birthday – we won't ask which. ....

Yrs, M.B.

1 *Two Visits to Denmark*, 1911.
2 Théophile (or Theodore) Marzials, poet and song writer, who met E.G. when they were both working at the British Museum.
3 Gosse's son (1879–1959). Doctor, naturalist and author.

COUNTESS BENCKENDORFF   The Lockyer Hotel, Plymouth
le 22 juin 1912

Je suis parti hier matin mais à cause de la grève nous avons du toucher à Plymouth.[1] ... Le bateau est, je crois, bon mais à cause de la grève il n'y a pas un seul vieux matelot à bord ... Très peu de passagers première classe. Une masse de steerage que je sens ne seraient jamais sauvés en cas de naufrage. L'idée du voyage me donne un terrible Aunt Sister.[2] J'ai beaucoup de livres avec moi. *La Grandeur et le Déclin de l'Empire Romain* de Ferrero, le nouveau livre d'Anatole France, *Fréderique le Grand* de Carlyle, quatre romans de Walter Scott, *L'Avènement de Bonaparte* de Vandal, *Napoléon à Sainte-Hélène* de Masson, les oeuvres de Platon, la poésie de Pushkin, Shakespeare, Dante, Racine, quatre histoires detectives, Aristote sur l'art drama-tique, quatre mauvais romans, un volume de Dumas père, la vie de Stead, les Évangiles, cinq romans de Marryat, un roman de Henry Kingsley. J'ai une très bonne cabine avec beaucoup de place. La mer est bleu et calme et en face le Devonshire tout scintillant de soleil comme dans mon enfance et comme dans votre tableau fait pour mon conte de fée.[3] Voir cette côte avec la route faite par mon père et les rochers, mes plages où je jouais comme enfant me donne un *ridge*[4] terrible. L'éclairage est tellement ce que c'était et ne ressemble à rien d'autre. ...

Je donnerais tout au monde pour être à Sosnofka ...

A vous, M.

1 This was the start of the journey that gave M.B. his material for *Round the World in Any Number of Days*, published in America in 1914 after large parts had appeared in the *Metropolitan Magazine*, N.Y. It was not published in England until 1919 when it was illustrated by Lord Basil Blackwood

(1870–1917), who had illustrated Hilaire Belloc's *Bad Child's Book of Beasts*. A list of the books M.B. read on the voyage is given on pp. 56–7 (collected edition).
2 A word from the Baring-Ponsonby language, meaning the shirking of a social duty, after one of the Grey family who never exerted herself and went to bed when the bell rang.
3 Refers to his childhood in Membland.
4 Depression.

EDMUND GOSSE   Placentinas, 47, Seville[1]
                                              14 April, 1913

My dear Chermaître,

I am I think intoxicated with beauty and feel I must write to you. I am writing to you from or rather in the gardens of the Alcazar, the gardens of the palace of the King. It is not the most comfortable place to write in; as I am balancing a few unwieldy leaves of a block on a very small book, on my knee, and I am sitting like Humpty Dumpty on a wall, a low wall. This garden is not only beautiful but it is inexplicable to me at least, miraculous, a thing I thought could not exist outside a fairy tale.

The paths are paved with red bricks and fringed with box hedges and low walls made of coloured tiles (old Moorish tiles) and in between the walls and paths are beds or rather 'closes' full of trees and flowers, peach trees and orange trees, which are now in blossom and whose sweetness comes to me in fitful and almost overpowering gusts, and yet on the topmost branches of the trees there are still oranges, bright and out of reach like the fruit in that little fragment of Sappho, on the topmost branches of all, so high that the pickers didn't forget it but couldn't reach it. The stiff symmetrical 'closes' are full of rose bushes, pink roses all in bloom, and purple irises (this letter has been interrupted here by two nurses and three children, a little boy of two who tried to jump into the fountain and a little child of one, whose mouth bled and now had to be washed. His name is Ramón.) And now three Germans have come with their Baedekers and hoarse guttural ejaculations, and two Frenchwomen with parasols and black hats, twittering with pleasure and wondering why I am writing on a wall with a fountain pen. And other frogs are croaking and the Cathedral bells are ringing for vespers and birds are singing and a little further off the lilac trees are out and the acacias and the daphne, and the geraniums and yellow roses climb on the walls and jessamine and cherry pie. What happens to the seasons here? Do they all come at once? Or does a fairy just descend with a wand and say to the flowers you must all blossom at once and go on blossoming? And ... in spite of the geraniums and the roses and in spite of all these flowers the main impression is one of greenery, green leaves, green hedges, green bushes, and dark sunburnt brick walls, 'annihilating all that's made to a green thought in a green shade'.[2] And a little Moorish summerhouse with white arches and tiled walls brilliant in colour and design, and every now and then an Andalusian gardener with a brown face and a great broad stiff hat, *sombrero ancho*, rugged and dignified, tasting of Flora and the country green and looking like a figure of Velazquez, comes strolling by and wishes you the good evening. And then many and various kinds of sweetnesses, the syringa, the orange blossom, the roses, come to one in puffs till one almost dies in aromatic pain. This is the garden where the sensitive plant grew;[3] and it is perhaps more wonderful, more extraordinary and more aromatic than that.

I have now shifted my position to a lower wall, almost on the level of the ground. In front of me is a high railing and through it I see the palace, a tower, some arches, and on the right a long rococo wall covered with a shell-like ornamentation of the bark of cork trees. ... I turn round and on the other side of me is a whole square of pink rose-bushes, very large and tall, out of which rise the orange trees in blossom. And through a cleft in the orange trees against the wall I can see a little patch of blue, light blue sky over a crenellated wall blazing in the sun, and on the nearer wall faded frescoes of pagan deities are framed in cork ornamentation. But this sweetness is now so overpowering I can't go on writing. Every minute the place grows lovelier and sweeter as the afternoon deepens. The tiles are strewn with fallen orange blossom and the nurse who is scolding little Ramón the baby has a sprig of orange blossom behind her ear against her black hair. And now the gardener passes and says to me with a smile, '*Trabajando?*' Working? Yes, one must be mad to write in such a garden.

Yrs, M.B.

It is so hot no blotting paper is necessary even in the shade.

1 M.B. had been seriously ill in January and had been operated on for an internal abscess. He was in Seville recovering, where he stayed with a painter friend M. de Bréal. The alcazar inspired him to write a sonnet; see *Collected Poems*.

2 Andrew Marvell, 'The Garden'.

3 Shelley, 'The Sensitive Plant'.

ARNOLD BENNETT   Sosnofka, Govt. of Tambov, Russia
                                                October 2, 1913

My dear Arnold,

I was delighted to get your letter yesterday. Aren't you suffering from self-mistrust engendered by great, continued and popular success? Don't bother about any generation thinking you old-fashioned. In the first place you are probably mistaking a clique for a generation. In the second place it does not matter. Don't bother about being praised by the wrong newspapers and publishers. Remember that there are always a certain number of people – especially among the young – who cannot bear to endorse a popular verdict.

> So much they scorn the crowd, that if the throng
> By chance go right, they purposely go wrong.[1]

Personally I think the popular verdict, the verdict of the crowd, is always right in the long run if you give it time. It may take a long time and it may go wrong at first but in the end it is always right, and if it goes right quickly and at once that is no sign that it is wrong. So cheer up ...

I am in Russia because I have got two book jobs to finish ... and I must be on the spot to do them. I shall certainly come and see you if I may directly I come back.

The house I am staying in is full of your books...

It takes Belloc ages to remember anybody's face. He is constantly unconsciously cutting people he has met.

Mes hommages les plus respectueux à Madame.

                                                Yours, M.B.

1 Pope, *Essay on Criticism*.

H. G. WELLS

[Sosnofka, Tambov]
October 4, 1913

My dear H. G.,

I am trying hard to read *The Passionate Friends* slowly.[1] I am trying hard to finish it at once. It is like trying to go down a watershute slowly or to appreciate an electric shock by degrees and the result is I have nearly finished it and it only came yesterday and there won't be a new book by H. G. Wells for at least a year.

Does criticism interest you? The kind of criticism which resolves itself into complaining of a book for not being something else has always seemed to me futile and in the case of this book I soon realized that it was an organic whole like a plum-pudding, to be taken or left, and that to complain of this and that in the framework was like saying why hasn't the plum-pudding got a crust and why isn't it filled with apples ...

The book, like all your books, stirred me, moved me, took me right out of myself, flashed pictures on my mind, opened out horizons, and touched me to the quick with stabs of insight and reality, and why shouldn't I write and thank you for all this – it isn't as you know an everyday experience! ...

If I could go to your literary kitchen and order what I liked for my next meal, I should order, amongst all sorts of side dishes about more planets, more accelerators (the retarder for instance), more machines, more beasts, another solid dish. I should like another such a novel, a pie this time. I leave the ingredients to you. Personally I should like the framework of the story to be in the third person, and I should like it very long. I daresay it is in the making or perhaps already made.

I should like you some day to make a study of Catholicism[2] – I daresay you think it is a kind of obscurantist whim or fad which no intelligent modern person could possibly take seriously but I don't think you would think that if you studied the question. One great truth about it burst on me last year in New Zealand when I was reading a book of Mallock's and which seemed to me to explain what had hitherto puzzled me in a million manifestations.[3] It is this (I am quoting Mallock as far as I remember what he says). That in England the popular conception of Catholicism has been so distorted by familiarity with Protestantism that the true conception of Catholicism is something foreign to the English. The Protestant clergy talk as if Rome were a

[84]

lapsed Protestant sect and are constantly attacking it for being false to doctrines that were never hers.

(And here I add, N. B., that it is not only the Protestant clergy but the Protestant-coloured agnostics, the Protestant-influenced politicians, statesmen, men of business, playwrights, novelists – Galsworthy, Bernard Shaw, as well as the Rev. Cope or the Rev. Surplice, and there are hints of it in your last books.) They fail to see that the difference which separates them, says Mallock – or words to that effect – is not in any special dogma but in the authority in which all dogmas root. Protestants basing their authority in the Bible think Catholics do also and abuse them for being traitors to their supposed profession. But the Roman Catholic Church's first doctrine is her own perpetual infallibility. She is inspired, she says, by the same spirit that inspired the Bible. The voice is equally the voice of God, and he goes on to say that looked on like this Rome must seem to Protestants a mass of superstitious dishonesty, and that this is the view that advanced thinkers have accepted. They have trusted the Protestants in nothing else but they have trusted them in this; they have taken the Protestants' word for it, that Protestantism is more reasonable than Catholicism, and they think that if they have destroyed the former they have *a fortiori* destroyed the latter.

This seems to me, for instance, precisely the point of view with regard to Catholicism of so high an intellect as Arthur Balfour,[4] or so vigorous a mind as Shaw's. They take it for granted that Catholicism includes not only the professions but the actual words of Protestantism. That is why any Englishman who wants to obtain a true view of Catholicism must begin by cancelling all the views that he has imbibed by tradition about it.

You may perhaps say, 'Why should I pay the slightest attention to this thing? I think it may contain points of interest but it is to me an exotic phenomenon, a game in which I am not interested, and why should I bother about its complicated rules – if I don't want to play that game?'

Well, what I would answer to that is that Catholicism is the only real living religion at this moment that is influencing mature humanity. That it is a gigantic fact, that no discoveries of science which shake Bible-founded Protestantism or any Bible-founded sect to its foundation, have the slightest effect on it. Its claim to infallibility is of such a nature when you understand it that no study of ecclesiastical history or of comparative mythology and no progress of criticism can possibly invalidate it.

This is what our people don't realize, because they don't realize the claim.

And apart from this, as a code of philosophy and morals it is worth study, and apart from this as a living thing which in its day from time to time is engaging intelligent thinkers in all the different countries of the world. These are some of the reasons I think it worthy of study.
...

Bless you, H. G.

Yrs, M.B.

1 Novel by Wells, published 1913.
2 In 1943 Wells published *Crux Ansata. An Indictment of the Roman Catholic Church*.
3 William Jurrell Mallock (1849–1923), author and satirist; wrote extensively against socialism and radicalism. M.B. did not list any of his books in *Round the World in Any Number of Days* amongst those he read on his voyage.
4 Arthur James Balfour (1848–1930), philosopher and statesman; Conservative prime minister 1902–5; O.M. 1916, cr. K.G. and earl 1922.

DAME ETHEL SMYTH   B.E.F., France
                                                 October 25, 1914
... I assure you when the troops arrived singing 'It's a long long way to Tipperary' at Maubeuge, after forced marches in the dark, it was one of the most tremendous moments I have ever experienced. The most tremendous. They swung up, or the tune swung them up a very steep hill over the ringing pavement and the French came out of their houses and threw flowers and fruit at them and gave them cigarettes, and they looked so young, so elastic and so invincibly cheerful, so unmixedly English, so tired and so fresh, and the thought of these people swinging on into horror undreamt of, the whole German army, came to me like the stab of a sword, and I had to go and hide in a shop, for the people not to see the tears rolling down my cheeks. I couldn't let my mind dwell on it for days after without the gulp in my throat coming back. I went to Mass this morning, and it was nice to think I was listening to the same words with the same gestures that Henry V and his 'contemptible little army' heard before and after Agincourt, and I stood between a man in khaki and a French Tommy and history flashed past like a jewelled dream.

G. K. CHESTERTON   H.Q., R.F.C.
                                                   May 24, 1915

My dear Gilbert,

It was a joy to see your name once more in *The Illustrated London News*. I have had a week of great anxiety and still greater grief. Lady Desborough's son Julian,[1] whom I have known since he was three years old, was very severely wounded in the head and it is a question whether he will live. I don't yet know – three days ago he was still in a critical condition – but I hope.

My greatest friend out here, who shared the same room with me from the beginning of the War, was killed on the 11th. His name was Barrington-Kennett. He was adjutant of the Flying Corps and the soul and spirit of it. Then he fell sick and the doctor forbade him to do any more office work and he was offered the command of a Flying Squadron but he refused it because he thought a Squadron Commander ought to fly and he had promised his wife to give up flying. He was a brilliant pilot and balloonist. So he went back to his regiment, the Grenadiers, and was shot in an attack. He was the kind of Englishman you could have transplanted to any epoch of our history to the adornment and advantage of that epoch, just as you could transplant a lyric of Robert Bridges[2] to the Elizabethan time. ... This has affected me more than anything that has happened. He was one of the finest characters I ever met, one of those characters Kipling has so often tried and in my opinion so lamentably failed to put on canvas, utterly unselfish, utterly devoted to his duty, very capable and very brave, and when I think of all the fun we had – however I don't know why I bore you with all this.

I read your last article. I suppose the Germans would say the military purpose of sinking the *Lusitania* was the destruction of the ammunition on board but you are right they are horrible, not terrible. You should see the names the soldiers put on their lorries and enormous traction engines which pull guns about, 'Melba', 'La Demi-Mondaine', 'Little Willy', 'Tired Tim', 'The Berlin Express'. I am full of hope and faith.

                                                   Yrs, M.B.

P.S. The articles of the Harmsworth Press are disgustingly mean and cowardly. 'Treasonable' is too exalted a term for them; I mean I think it would do Harmsworth too great an honour to try him for <u>treason</u>, just as certain Souls weren't allowed to go to Hell... He ought to be treated as a boy who throws mud and I am sorry the pillory is abolished.[3]

1 Julian Grenfell (1888–1915) soldier and poet, who died of his wound.
2 Robert Seymour Bridges (1844–1930), poet laureate 1913, O.M. 1929.
3 The Harmsworth brothers (later Lords Northcliffe and Rothermere) at this time controlled and influenced the editorial policy of *The Times*, the *Daily Mail*, the *Daily Mirror*, and the *Evening News*. They were running a campaign of dissatisfaction against Lord Kitchener, the Secretary of State for War.

G. K. CHESTERTON   [H.Q., R.F.C.]
June 5, 1915

My dear Gilbert,

There are many things I should like to write about in the public press at this moment, only being on active service I am not allowed to write about such things and <u>deliberately</u> at the beginning of the War I sought for that position, the one tiny sacrifice one could make. This is private and for you only... However, not being able to write, there is something I would give anything you would write for me if you agree with it and that is a short homily to the effect that people have forgotten the meaning of some quite elementary words... One of these things and one of those words is TREASON. People have forgotten what that means and the thing is present with us and people having forgotten what it is deal with it as tho' it were a taste in music or an effort of the Stage Society. For instance there is the 'Society for Democratic Control', to which, I am ashamed to say, belong one or two people I know and like. They do not realize that what they are partaking in is treason because they have forgotten what treason means. They send letters to the parents whose sons have died in duty and fighting, gloating over their loss and urging them to stop the war. Some people think – and I believe with good grounds – that the Society is financed by German money but the point is even if it was, the majority of the members would never find it out, so blunted is their sense of the fundamental wrongness and rightness of the question.

Another instance. Frank Harris,[1] as soon as the War begins, declares he is and has been for years an American subject and writes articles of passionate hate against England which he now republishes in a book, hatred of England and praise of Germany: and Arnold Bennett, writing about it in *The Daily News*, treats it <u>on the same plane</u> as if he were discussing the <u>cussedness</u> of an amiable and 'naughty' faddist. He talks of his 'tiresome' anti-Englishness. He doesn't seem to see that that kind of thing makes or should make a great gulf and that the man ought to be beyond the pale. These people talk of the 'sincerity' of these people. I have no doubt they [are] sincere. I have also no doubt Judas Iscariot was sincere and Brutus, whom Dante makes his colleague and 'Kamerad' in the Jaws of Lucifer, was certainly sincere, but why is he there? Because <u>he was a traitor</u>. And one is either a traitor or one isn't. One would think to hear people talk you could be a traitor <u>in some respects</u> and a patriot in other respects. Now, to my blunter mind, anybody who, when their country is in peril, does anything, either by word, thought or deed which is of assistance to the enemy is a traitor to his country and deserves a traitor's death, whatever his motive, howsoever burning his sincerity. Do you agree? If so, I wish you would use your powerful pen to point it out.

Yrs, M.B.

1 James Thomas (Frank) Harris (1856–1931), author, editor and adventurer. He had spent much of his youth in America and returned there at the beginning of the war. He had been writing pro-German articles in *The New York Sun* and his book *England or Germany* (1915) caused much indignation. He blamed the war on the English aristocracy and said that the sinking of a few food ships would bring about a revolution, when the Government could admit defeat and England would become a third-rate power.

LADY DESBOROUGH   [H.Q., R.F.C., B.E.F.]
25 September 1915

Dearest,

It rained all the afternoon but at a quarter to six I looked out of the office window and to my astonishment saw that the gap of sky between the trees was all gold, and turning right round and looking through the window over the chimney piece that faces due East, I saw in the watery greyness a faint blush and a high rainbow soaring into the top of the sky. I at once went out and walked up the hill towards the flying ground.

Over the trees at the top of the hill which were dark green and almost black, the watery greyness was all gold, with a soft line fading higher into a pink radiance. The stubble under the trees in the foreground to

the right of the road was bright and burnished, and a grey horse plod-
ded slowly backwards and slowly forwards ploughing. It was too dark
in spite of the lightness to see the ploughman.

In the East there was a pile of huge round clouds, white against the
greyness and soft, and the grey church tower against them looked like
the shape made out of a different sort of cloud. In the distance one
heard the thud of guns and a soldier walked past in khaki, wet and
muddy, and it didn't seem like autumn and it didn't seem like summer
and still less like sunset or like spring but like the unearthly dawn of a
new season and a strange glory.

Yrs, Maur.

LADY DESBOROUGH   H.Q., R.F.C., B.E.F.
                                                              1.10.15
Dearest,

The newspapers are having slowly but surely a deadly disintegrating
effect.

(a) In the past by exaggerating, boasting. When the fighting at Ypres
was going on, they had huge headlines saying 'Enemy hurled back', and
what people seem to forget is that these newspapers reach Headquarters on the day they come out and the Divisions the next morning and
the trenches within 18 hours. So that the thinning line reading such
things and knowing that they were holding on by the skin of their teeth
were not encouraged.

(b) By exaggerated panic and depression about the fighting everywhere, especially in *The Times* and the *Daily Mail*. Even the people
who pay no attention and disbelieve insensibly have their minds gradually coloured by the press. I am conscious of this process myself.

(c) By widespread and often utterly unfounded criticism on everything and everybody, starting with K.[1] This of course has a disastrous
effect.

(d) By long detailed accounts by war correspondents of operations
while those operations are still proceeding and before their ultimate
issue is certain. It passes my understanding that this should be allowed,
i.e. to talk of 'German collapse' etc. when for all you know on the very
next day they may be preparing a terrific counter attack. I cannot see
why these accounts should not be held over until the operations are

finished. The French would not and do not dream of allowing this. They know the effect it could have on their people.

(e) By headlines which are nearly always thumping lies. And silly. 'German Strategy thwarted'. How can they know it was thwarted when they can't possibly know what the intended strategy was? Apart from the Daily Press there are hundreds of small technical newspapers with regard to every branch of the service which consist entirely of destructive criticism on the way that particular branch is managed and of attacks on the various people responsible. These newspapers are read with avidity. The criticisms they contain cannot help being based on an incomplete and insufficient knowledge of the facts: the people who know the facts are very rightly not allowed to answer. But again, I should think we ought to do every possible thing we can to beat the Huns, and if so why is this allowed? I will give you a small instance. There is a newspaper called *The Aeroplane* dealing with aeronautics. It discusses every detail of the whole air service both in the field and at home in 'fearless old fashion', attacking everyone right and left, sometimes saying very sensible things, sometimes very silly things but the thing that hits you in the face is that you see they are not in possession of the whole truth, the complete facts, and this makes their whole judgement *pécher par la base*, crumble in its fundamentals. [Here] is a small instance. One day there was a fierce attack on the Home Flying Authorities (it happened to be Trenchard[2]) for sending a 'young and inexperienced' pilot to Liverpool to fly a new machine. The pilot happened to be Hawker.[3] A professional almost as good as Hamel, one of the 4 or 5 best pilots in the world – they withheld his name on purpose because they didn't want a fuss made about it and for other excellent reasons.

What is true about this newspaper is true about a hundred others. And nearly all these technical newspapers contain details which must be of value to the enemy.

I wish you would talk about this to all the influential people you know. The Ks, the AJBs, the George Curzons, etc.[4] Harmsworth could I believe be damned if all leading men were simply to write to some other newspaper instead of writing to *The Times*.

Yours, M.

1 Horatio Herbert Kitchener, Earl Kitchener of Khartoum (1850–1916). Field-Marshal. K.G., O.M., P.C., etc. At the time he was Secretary of State for War.

2 Col. Hugh (Montague) Trenchard (1873–1956) was appointed G.O.C., R.F.C. on 19 August. Subsequently Marshal of the R.A.F. Cr. Baron 1930, Viscount 1936, O.M. 1951. He became a close friend of M.B. who was best man at his wedding. See M.B.'s *Flying Corps Headquarters 1914–1918* and *Trenchard* by Andrew Boyle (1962).

3 Squadron Commander Lanoe George Hawker (1890–1916), V.C., D.S.O.

4 A. J. Balfour was at the time First Lord of the Admiralty and George Curzon, a former Viceroy of India, cr. Marquess Curzon of Kedleston, Lord Privy Seal.

LADY JULIET DUFF

H.Q., R.F.C.
9.12.15[1]

> Petite pomme d'api
> Take your pen and write to me.
> Sweetest apple on the tree.
> Prends ta plume, O ma mie,
> If thy pen displeaseth thee,
> Write on a machine to me;
> I am sad exceedingly,
> Far away beyond the sea
> Far from my felicity;
> Loin de toi, ma mort, ma vie,
> Quelle scie que la vie!
> Toute bonne, toute jolie,
> I am like a hungry bee,
> Hungry for the taste of thee;
> Mon amour et mon amie;
> Take your pen and write to me,
> Juliette, je t'en prie.
> Je suis ton fidèle ami,
> Petite pomme d'api,
> Take your pen and write to me.
>
> Yours forever, M.B.

1 M.B. wrote almost daily to Lady Juliet and often several times a day. He was intensely busy at the time and it was a way of relaxing. A delightful selection from these – *Dear Animated Bust: Letters to Lady Juliet Duff. France 1915–1918* – was published, with an introduction by Margaret FitzHerbert, in 1981.

EDWARD MARSH   [H.Q., R.F.C., B.E.F.]
                                                No date [early 1916]

My dear E.,

No, it is not quite what I meant about translatability. I accept your creed 'in toto', that the best poetry should be incommunicable, and that the charm of a thing being said in one particular way should make it necessary for you to learn the language. I think that is the true Faith. But I think that all poetry, all real poetry, fulfils that condition. I think that all poetry, all real poetry is untranslatable. I think <u>very great</u> poetry, <u>the best of all poetry</u>, even if it only keeps it up for a line, while fulfilling this condition, gives readers the illusion that they could translate it, if only they knew how. And tempts people to try and to fail and even in failing something remains; the reader of the translation sees that there is something better in the original, the reader, for instance, of '*Ille mi par esse*'.[1]

But there is another category which, though exquisite in itself, doesn't give people this temptation, because it is too local and not universal enough, not only in meaning but not universal enough in possible future alien style. Of the tempting lines Dante is full. Dante is untranslatable. You must learn Italian to appreciate him. But his lines seem so perfectly obvious in their pictorial, musical, meaningful, atmospheric beauty that everybody is lured into thinking he can be translated. And even in the failures something subsists, if it is very well done, just as something of Sappho subsists in Catullus... Rossetti has always seemed to me ... to be like the almond on the top of cakes, indigestible, unless you are young enough to eat it and devour it in chunks. But there is always a second childhood and my second childhood enables me to nibble at that which ten years ago I rejected. ...

                                                Yours, M.B.

1 Catullus, *Carmina* no. 51.

LADY JULIET DUFF   H.Q., R.F.C.
                                                January 1, 1916

Chère Jumelle,

... I returned from Italy last night. It was, my very dear, one of the most exhausting journeys I have ever done. We motored all day to Paris then after a hurried dinner we rushed to the Gare de Lyon and thence rushed to Turin. Then the next morning we got up at five and went by train, changing five times till the train stopped altogether. Then we hired a motor and drove across the Ticino, and for all I know the Rubicon and the Tiber and Lake Maggiore, through Lombarda and Novara and Arona to Gellerata, where the Italians learn how to fly.

There we inspected the Caproni machine in a shed and thence we drove to Malpensa, where Dante was born and Virgil died, and there we were introduced to forty-five Flying Officers, who each one said his name and clicked his heels. Then we had luncheon. At the end of luncheon the Captain in command made a speech about delicious England and adorable English people and I made a speech about divine Italians. Then an Italian pilot, myself and the man with me went up in the Caproni into the sky. Into the grey, misty, sunless, lampless, sullen, unpeopled sky. And as the machine climbed, the curtains of Heaven were rent asunder, and through and over oceans of mist and rolling clouds, naked, majestic, white, shining and glorious rose the Alps, like a barrier, and at our feet, dark, as a raven's wing, loomed the waves of Lake Maggiore, fringed with foaming breakers, and the earth was outspread beneath us like a brown and purple carpet. And we climbed and banked and climbed and banked and climbed and far beneath us a little Maurice Farman fluttered like a white dove. Then suddenly the three engines stopped buzzing and we turned and banked and turned and dived and turned sheer and steep till we gently rolled on to the ground.

Then we spent a few hours in technical conversation and then we went by train to Milan and dined. After dinner we nearly missed the train and finally got back to Turin at midnight. The next day we started for Paris.

A Frenchman sitting next to us in the train whom I knew said to me: 'Il y a seulement 14 personnes qui voyagent maintenant et on est sûr de les rencontre tous. Vous êtes un des 14.' Castelnau was likewise one of the quatorze.

We reached Paris the next morning and thence hither in the fastest motor n the world.

Au revoir, ma libellule,

Ton Zo-Zou-Zimimini

P.S. LET US WRITE TO EACH OTHER EVERY DAY THIS YEAR. IT IS ONLY FUN WRITING IF ONE WRITES EVERY DAY.

This letter is reproduced by M.B. in *Flying Corps Headquarters 1914–1918* (pp. 118–19, collected edition) and also by Lord Birkenhead in his posthumous *The Five Hundred Best English Letters* (1931). In neither book is the recipient named and the letter as published differed from the original, which is as above and was reproduced in *Dear Animated Bust* (*op. cit.*).

EDWARD MARSH Headquarters, Royal Flying Corps, B.E.F., France
January 26th, 1916

My dear Eddy,

... One point which it may be useful to rub in is that no change in direction, personnel, policy, organisation or anything else would <u>now</u> be effectual in accelerating the production of one single part, pin or bolt in one single engine or machine, as all the available brains, hands and feet are working as hard and as fast as they possibly can to turn out machines and engines.

The disadvantages from which we now suffer (and which are not at all what the public imagine) are the result of there being at the outbreak of the war no plant to make metal stampings, which were all made in Belgium, no means of making magnetos which, as you know, being Bosch were made in Germany. The same is true of those shell fuses which were made in Switzerland.

That no provision of this kind existed then was due to the refusal of the Treasury to provide money for that purpose (they had been asked and asked and asked), so you can either blame the Treasury for want of foresight or the German Emperor for making war, or both.

That the Flying Service, although in its infancy at the beginning of the war, was nevertheless not unprepared and certainly excellently organized and directed is proved by the fact that we took the initiative and gained superiority in the air at the very outset of the war. (In spite of our fundamental unreadiness for war compared with the fundamental readiness for war of the Germans.)

That we are not in such a very bad way at present is proved by the fact that the initiative is still being maintained although the German machines have greatly improved.

Our supply of fast machines is daily increasing and yesterday a new Scout outflew and outclimbed the fastest French bullet monocoque monoplane Moraine... which is as fast as a Fokker.

With regards to complaints of pilots about our policy – i.e. the policy of (a) crossing the line daily (b) long distance reconnaissances – remember one thing: the pilots are the worst judges of policy because they don't know what the policy consists of nor what is necessary to it. They don't know <u>why</u> nor the plan into which it fits. This is solely a question for G.H.Q. and the C.G.S. They know the risk; they know the possible loss, it is for them to judge whether the information gained is worth it. If they think it is worth it – <u>necessary</u> – the work must be done however dangerous.

But one thing should be noted: there is a great difference between long distance reconnaissances and merely crossing the line. The former requires engines with an increased supply of petrol. ... Were the latter, the mere crossing of the line, to be given up, it is difficult to believe that the moral effect would not be one of great exhilaration to the Germans and great depression to our own pilots, <u>as it would mean abandoning the initiative</u>.

Another reason why it is dangerous to listen to pilots: they, and especially those in England, only know part of what is happening and generally know nothing at all of the supply question, of what is being done, and what is projected for the future. Take three pilots and each will give you a different opinion on the merits of one machine (of which they have had practical experience). Also I have heard them call and call and call and pray for a type of machine and then when they got it say it was useless... They are in some respects like prima donnas discussing an orchestra. The only people who can give you a fair opinion are experienced Wing Commanders... What the public says is fantastic nonsense.

Yours, M.B.

PROFESSOR SPENCER WILKINSON   Headquarters, Royal Flying Corps, B.E.F. France

23.3.16

CONFIDENTIAL

Dear Wilkinson,

I have just read your letter in *The Times* with regard to the Air question.[1]

I think it may possibly interest you to receive a few impressions which I have gathered since the beginning of the war. They have at any rate the merit of being firsthand. And as better than anyone you know my limitations you will be able to take them for what they are worth.

I have been with the Headquarters of the R.F.C. ever since the Advance party of that Corps arrived in France in August 1914.

1 The first great lesson I have learnt during this war and one which I think applies more especially to aircraft, and all that is concerned with it, is the extreme danger of forming an opinion on a partial knowledge of the facts. One is often told the truth by people who have first hand experience. One is seldom told the whole truth, owing to the fact that people don't know it. Again the conclusions at which the personnel engaged in fighting in the air arrive as a result of their experience are often diametrically at variance.

Thirdly, there is a great deal of information circulated which is simply untrue; although sometimes it proceeds from what should be good sources and is due not to any desire to mislead but to the ignoring or the ignorance of what are essential factors in the case.

Fourthly, there is the gossip of the inaccurate; and the biased grievances of the discontented, the disappointed, and the inefficient; the slanders of the envious, and the petty spite of those who have been found wanting and ejected. All this has a wide circulation.

It is said that the public interest in aircraft which has now become of so feverish a nature is a healthy sign. It is a pity this interest did not manifest itself in a greater degree before the war; in that case the Government might have been compelled to make the preparations which the Air authorities thought necessary in the case of a war. But the public at large – and who knows that better than you? – did not believe in the necessity of preparing for war. The military Command which dealt with aircraft did. And the proof of this is our acknowledged superiority in the air at the outset of the war.

That is one reason why the present attacks on men like General Henderson, who realized the importance of aircraft long before the war began and did all they could to advance its progress in every kind of way, are not only dastardly but misguided.

2 The chief point which is of interest now is I think this: what are our disadvantages in the air compared to the forces of the enemy and how far can they be remedied and how far are they being remedied? But connected with this question is the further question how far was it the

military Command at the beginning of the war, and before it, responsible for such disadvantages as may exist?

The chief advantage the Germans have over us is in the matter of engines: not only in the <u>kind</u> of engine but the actual <u>material</u> of which the engines are made. As you know, before the war the whole world bought its Bosch magnetos in Germany. Therefore, when the war began it was necessary for us not only to make engines but to make the plant for making them. This eventuality was foreseen by those in authority but in asking the Treasury then (which was done) to take steps and provide money for making things which would not be forthcoming if we went to war with Germany, one had had as much chance of being heeded as if one had asked them to endow a college for teaching canaries Greek. And you know this better than anyone. It was all one could do to get them not to disband the Navy.

Why are the German engines superior? Largely because of the superiority in composition of German steel. They do it better just as they make better lenses, not because they have better material to work with but because they have studied and mastered the question.

Another drawback. Metal stampings before the war were made in Belgium. All I have said with regard to the engines applies to this. Only it should be remembered that the same kind of metal stampings do not serve for every type of machine, so that as new machines are invented and adopted, new stampings and metal fittings become necessary, and to make these it is necessary to make the plant.

Therefore, the record of our supply of material since the war began is a long record of the manufacture of bricks without straw against time, and the further hindrance of strikes and active, actual warfare.

One point you will often hear from the semi-expert and in that vague and not altogether high-minded and disinterested world of civil aeronautics is that had the Government paid more attention to private firms we should have started on equal terms with the Germans at the very beginning. Some months ago an R.F.C. pilot said to me that at the beginning of the war we had the chance of having Vickers fighting machines and had that been the case our pilots would have shot the Germans like sparrows. Well the truth is that we did have that chance and that the machines were ordered but the pilot left out one essential fact which entirely altered the whole question. And I am convinced he was unaware of this fact. The Vickers machine is worked by the Gnome monosoupape engine. This engine was at the beginning of the war totally unreliable. It was only by this time last year that a Vickers with monosoupape became reliable enough for use. And even now they are not satisfactory and cases of engine failure occur daily.

It is not true to say that private firms have been neglected.

It is not true to say that the R.A.F. factory has a monopoly of the supply of engines for the R.F.C.

It is true to say that everything has been done and is being done daily to obtain the maximum quantity of the best French and even Spanish engines.

It is true to say that everything is being done to make English firms manufacture those French and Spanish engines which experience has shown to be valuable and reliable in England.

Is this an easy matter? Alas! it is not! Does a firm that has hitherto manufactured monosoupape Gnomes which have been proved to be useless like to be told to manufacture 110 Le Rhônes? No it does not. Does the firm believe in this superiority which has been proved by experience? No it does not. Does it show alacrity? No, the very reverse. Does he say he will have to manufacture new tools? He does. Does he say this will take a short time? He does not. But can it be done? Well, the answer is that it is done in France and done quickly, tools and all.

3 The public in discussing the subject of aeroplanes do not realize that the work required from aircraft in war is of different kinds and that for these different kinds of work different machines are necessary. So that a machine which could be rightly stigmatized as being useless for one kind of work might none the less be still fully satisfactory for another kind of work.

As you probably know, the work of aircraft consists of co-operation with the artillery (perhaps the most important of all), photography, bomb dropping, in addition to reconnaissance. I have sometimes heard the Air Command abused for using so many machines for reconnaissance. But this, as you will be the first to realize, is a matter which concerns the Higher Command. If the Higher Command wants certain information it has to be got. But to go back to the main point, the variety of machines necessary or possible to be employed for the various kinds of work. This is often a source of most misguided, unsound and unfair criticism.

People will say what is the use of our having or of our still employing a machine like the B.E. which is no good or distinctly at a disadvantage as a fighter? Well, machines which are employed in this work do not as a rule come in for much fighting, as their work is done, for the most part, only just over the line. And the French are now setting apart for this work the 80 h.p. Maurice Farman, a machine we have long ago discarded as being too slow for practical work. It is too slow for scouting, reconnaissance, bomb dropping. The French find it is not too slow for artillery work. And indeed, this is a conclusion which they have arrived at quite recently. Well if the Maurice Farman 80 h.p. can do this work, much more can the B.E. 2c do so.

I have no wish to minimize our disadvantages. The Germans have much more powerful and more reliable engines which enable them to build heavier machines in which nothing which makes it easier and more comfortable for the pilot to fight is sacrificed to lightness. Therefore it is easier for them to fight in their machines. They are for daily work. It is not necessary to sacrifice anything. Further their engines are more reliable. There have been hardly any cases (I think only one or two) of the Germans suffering from engine failure over our lines. We have lost many machines from engine failure over the German lines. German pilots attribute this to the superiority of their mechanics. How far they are right here, I don't know.

Is anything being done to remedy our disadvantage in this respect and to give us a fighting machine which shall be a match in speed and reliability with the German machines? I need hardly say that this is not a question which has only just and suddenly occurred to those who are responsible. For months and months we have been clamouring for reliable and powerful engines and fighting machines. Rolls-Royce is making engines and we get a certain supply of excellent Le Rhône engines from the French and a certain supply of good fighting and very fast machines from the French Morane firm, who are further experimenting for us. We hope to get machines from the Nieuport firm also, whose machines have already proved a terror to the Germans at Verdun.

One word about the Fokker which, as so often happens, has taken the fancy of the British public because it has got a name. The Fokker is an exact copy of the French Morane monoplane. With a powerful engine put in it. We have a machine as fast if not faster than the Fokker.

But our type of machine which does the same kind of work which the Fokker does for the Germans – namely to wait till the enemy comes over and then to climb at top speed and shoot at him – is not quite so fast as the Fokker. We are obliged to use the machine which is as fast as he for other work, namely reconnaissance.

4 Another point which the public seem to overlook altogether is the fact that the R.F.C. is not a body of independent amateurs or athletes but a part of the British Army; that its pilots and observers are officers and command and maintain discipline; that its mechanics are private soldiers; that it forms part of a larger organisation and that this fact has many consequences which I need not point out to you. For instance, because a man is a star pilot it does not necessarily follow that he will be a good squadron commander. Because a man is a good rigger it does not follow he will be a possible Flight Sergeant. And this applies to the larger question you see so often discussed. Because a man is a good or has been a good pilot there is no reason [to suppose] that he will necessarily be a good Brigadier, a good organizer, tactician, strategist or General. Any more than a good tenor or violinist would necessarily make a good conductor for an orchestra or a good actor or good producer. Indeed very often the contrary is the case.

But when they say in the House of Commons that the Brigadiers (among them is one of the finest pilots in the world – Salmond[2]) are men who know nothing of flying, they are simply talking nonsense, and the same applies to Squadron Commanders. It is an interesting point that the Germans do not allow their Squadron Commanders to fly themselves. Ours are allowed to fly under certain conditions and with certain limitations.

5 The question of dual service: Army and Navy. The French have the great advantage of only having one service. Why can't we do this? Because I suppose England is an island and we must defend our coastline, which is a large order.

In our fighting area in France, the Navy has some seaplanes which are used for naval gunnery work and a certain number of stray machines which, though under the control of Dover, are used for haphazard expeditions in a haphazard way. Bombing. Is the existence of this duality a disadvantage? I think without any doubt. Is there rivalry between the two services? I would say not between the actual pilots but between the two Departments which look after the rival interests. There is. Just as there was in olden times that disastrous rivalry that lost us battles.

Is there a remedy?

The only chance of one would be in a separate and higher authority which could define the duties of each service and allot to each the necessary means to perform those duties. The difficulty is to find someone capable of doing this. If you get a clever politician, he will simply be at sea. If you get a soldier who knows what it is about, the Navy won't have him; if you get a sailor who knows, the Army won't have him.

What you want is a man strong enough to knock the heads of the two parties together and, without being an expert, knowledgeable enough to realize the nature of the questions at issue and the difficulties that have to be met. Does such a man exist? Will he be found? I devoutly hope so. Lord, I believe; help thou my unbelief.

The Derby Committee[3] is I am convinced no solution. It is an arena in which the Army and Navy fight presided over by good intentions and common sense hampered by invincible ignorance.

6 The influence of untrained civilian opinion for good and evil.

This is I am convinced a most important point. Public opinion goes off at half-cock. It cannot be trained. It is inflamed by the Press and fed with gossip. (Of the most fantastic kind.) Its influence acting on always ignorant and often pusillanimous politicians may be disastrous.

I will give you an instance. At the beginning of the war the French Flying Corps was commanded by General Hirschauer.[4] There were no two opinions about his capacity, his integrity and his knowledge of the subject. He was got rid of by intrigue.

The change was so manifestly for the worse that he was brought back. The political intrigue fostered by private firms who put (surprising thing!) their own interests before those of their country, got rid of him again. A civilian Minister was appointed in his stead. An honest man, and not a stupid man, but who frankly confessed he knew nothing about it. Work came to a standstill while the Minister was studying the elements of the case.

The Germans went on fighting and building and fighting. They had no time to wait till M. Besnard's education was completed. Result: a renewed agitation and the dismissal of M. Besnard. In his place General

Hirschauer was not restored (and I doubt if he ever will be, if he will ever consent, unless he is given a free hand all along the line). An officer was put in his place who, though good, was not the best choice available.

I regard this episode as equivalent to a German victory. Were those officers now in the Command of our Army Flying Corps in England and France replaced by stray persons at the bidding of politicians influenced by public opinion, I should regard it as a still greater German victory and I know the Germans would also.

On the other hand, I think there is a want of unity in control owing to the question of the defence of England and the fighting in France. I think the question has not been solved and I believe it could be solved if those who do the work were allowed to direct it. In a word, if the separate duties could be clearly defined and then those uncharged with those duties enabled to perform them; and if any such arrangement and definition once arrived at were rigidly adhered to.

Yours sincerely,
Maurice Baring

P.S. May I tell how deeply I felt for you in your personal loss in the war?[5] Most of my friends have been killed and most of the sons of my best friends. Many of them in this Corps. But I do not grudge them nor do I think there have been in the Corps cases of casualties that could have been avoided, more than happens in war.

Our pilots have been blamed for their adventurous spirit and the Command blamed for allowing it to have play, and for allowing them to go over the lines so much. Believe me, the answer is if we don't do it the Germans do, and if we then cease, it seriously affects the morale of our men. That high morale is the result of the daring and pluck shown in the past. Of course I think everything ought to be done to make our material as good as possible. I believe all that is possible is being done and that the only unsatisfactory question is the want of unity of control and a definite policy for the two services as I have already explained at length.

Incidentally, I should like to tell you that without any exaggeration I consider General Trenchard who commands the R.F.C. at present, out here, one of the biggest men I have ever come across, with something very like genius for getting work done and inspiring those under him, and with powers of organisation and a combination of large ideas with a minute eye and memory for detail and a fine discrimination for men that I have not seen I won't say equalled, but even approached in our Army. I happen to know this opinion is shared by the French who have seen him at work. So whether he remains here or works in England, I shall feel certain that only good can come of it.

And were anything outside to occur to diminish his powers or his influence, I should feel, as I have already said, that the Germans had won a victory.

M.B.

Billing's[6] remarks about General Henderson made me blush with shame.

1 This letter is evidently misdated as Spencer Wilkinson's letter 'Bungling by Ignorance' had been published in *The Times* on 25 March. It called for a strong administration for the R.F.C.
2 John Maitland Salmond (1881–1968). He had been flying since 1912. D.S.O. 1914, K.C.B. 1919, G.C.B. 1931, etc. He had joined the Army in 1901 and transferred to the R.F.C. in 1912. In 1918 he took over command of the R.F.C. in the field from Trenchard. In 1933 he became the second officer to hold the rank of Marshal of the Royal Air Force, the first having been Trenchard, whom he also succeeded at Chief of the Air Staff. In 1924 he married as his second wife Hon. Monica Grenfell, d. of Lord Desborough, making a further link with M.B.
3 Set up under Lord Derby to settle the conflicting interest of the Army and the Navy.
4 Auguste Edouard Hirschauer (1857–1943).
5 Lieutenant E.S. Wilkinson, R.F.C., son of the Professor, was reported in *The Times* of 3 February 1916 as having been killed flying.
6 N. Pemberton Billing (1880–1948), R.N.A.S. 1914–16. Retired and contested Mile End in support of strong air policy. M.P. (Ind.) East Herts. 1916–21. See Boyle, p. 174.

LADY JULIET DUFF   H.Q., R.F.C.

27.2.16

Blighty

I want to go to Blighty, for I do
Love Blighty more than any foreign land;
I want to see the shingle and the sand,
And Battersea, Vauxhall and Waterloo.

I want to hear the noises of the Strand;
Through the red fog I want to see a barge
Move slowly down the river, looming large;
I want to hear the music of the band.
I want to see the children at their play,
Feeding the ducks upon the Serpentine;
I want to hear the barrel-organs bray,
When the wet sunset in a narrow mews,
Reflected, makes the pavement puddles shine,
And ragamuffins yell the racing news.

The following week M.B. sent a version of this to G.K.Chesterton, in which 'the music of' is inserted before 'barrel-organs' in line 11 (metrically quaint!), and 'wet' becomes 'red' in line 12.

DESMOND MacCARTHY   H.Q., R.F.C., B.E.F., France
                                     26.3.16

My dear Desmond,

... This is what I think happens to Vernon [Lee] and her friends. ... She couldn't <u>quarrel with me</u> because it takes two to make a quarrel and I simply won't. I am very fond of her. But I always thought her the victim of a too subtle intellect and I always thought that whenever she denigrated the human beings I knew, she was frankly talking nonsense. As for instance when she said that Countess Benckendorff was a person who lived by half hours. Here is the whole material for a whole story by Henry James but it is farcical in this connection, an application as farcical as if one were to say that Hillary [Belloc] was a person to whom beer and the telephone were the blots on civilisation and the sores and plague-spots of modern existence. Or when she said that Ethel Smyth's singing was not music but 'a fine intellectual combustion'...

Did I ever tell you the story of the Wells dinner party? Wells asked Vernon to dinner. He is a comparatively old friend of hers. At her request he also asked me whom she had not seen for many years. He also asked Hillary. He also asked Haynes[1] who was his near neighbour and always did dine there on Sundays or Mondays. There happened to be an American about, one of those Americans who write philosophy without knowing what words mean and are guided by the sound only.

A nice man who had written some entirely meaningless books. He was given an introduction to Wells and, as he was to be in London for a few days only, Wells asked him too.

The table was arranged thus. Mrs Wells sat at the head of the table; on her right sat the American, then Vernon, then Hillary, then Haynes, then Wells, then Mrs Haynes, then myself, then Mrs Wells.

Hillary thought Vernon 'a good woman'. Vernon thought Hillary like a French *curé* who feeds at the *table d'hôte* at Dijon. She was enraged (a) because there was anyone else there besides Wells and me (Wells had told her I was coming), (b) because the American was next to her (whom she brutally ignored), (c) – and this is the only point of the story – because Haynes was there. She explained to me the next day that Wells had asked Haynes to give a stamp of Bourgeois respectability to an otherwise Bohemian party for the sake of the American!

She left after dinner in a pet and came to me the next day to tell me that the English were a fundamentally uncivilized race and the chief of the barbarians was Wells for having concocted such a party. And chiefly for having dared to ask an American and especially for having asked what she called the family solicitor!! This was Haynes! *J'avais beau dire* that Haynes was an old friend of Wells, of Hillary and of mine. It was no use. A whole elaborate theory was built on this.

Yrs, M.B.

1 Edmund Sidney Pollock Haynes (1877–1949), a noted London solicitor specializing in divorce. Brackenbury Scholar of Balliol College. A well-known intellectual and author of many books.

DESMOND MACCARTHY   H.Q., R.F.C., B.E.F., France
4.6.16

My dear Desmond,

I have been reading in the *New Witness* and the *New Statesman* your discussion with G.B.S. and Cecil Chesterton's discussion with G.B.S. about the Gospels.¹

Do you remember a sentence of Renan's where he said, *Quiconque voudrait reécrire les Évangiles* would prove *qu'il ne les entendait pas* or words to that effect? They are quoted by Matthew Arnold who adds that Renan was right to reconsider his decision.

And yet surely the *Vie de Jésus* is a failure if ever there was one. It doesn't solve the mystery, if Christ was only a man, of how and why such an astounding thing could happen, and the portrait of *ce charmant jeune homme roulant d'extase en extase* is not convincing and obviously the portrait of a Frenchman.

Again, Matthew Arnold describes Jesus Christ as a very cultured Don who is imploring people to realize that the Germans aren't stupid and that material success isn't the end all and be all and that *The Daily Telegraph* writes badly. Oscar Wilde on the other hand in *De Profundis* and *The Soul of Man* shows clearly that he was an artist, an artist in life, whose morality was all sympathy, and Gilbert Chesterton in *Orthodoxy* makes him into a virulent Anti-Dreyfusard who goes up on to the mountain to have a hearty laugh.

Whereas G.B.S. shows clearly that he was a witty Bohemian who would have written plays had there been a Stage Society near. Now given the fact that the existence of this person changed the whole face of the world, all this is very difficult to explain.

If, that is to say, the man was only a man.

Some explanation is necessary. You have either to say 'Yes, but he was a <u>very good</u> man.' Or that he was mad, went mad. Neither explanation [is] adequate.

Because no other very good man has [had] quite the same effect. Nobody, for instance, has believed that Socrates or even Buddha or Mahomet was God and madmen have not inspired people to die for them rather than deny them.

On the other hand you have the Church which claims to have been founded by that Person and claims the Gospels as the title deeds of her estate and an uninterrupted tradition from the days of Christ and his contemporaries. To be in fact the representative of the Divine on earth. If you admit that this claim is substantiated, the whole matter is simple, for the Church's version of the whole matter is drawn up in a clear and definite doctrine called the Church catechism which gives a clear and logical explanation of the facts. In fact <u>the</u> only clear and coherent explanation of the facts.

But this, you will point out, entails believing that Christ was God. And you will say this is difficult. I admit the difficulty. But I maintain that it is not more difficult than it is difficult for you and G.B.S. or anyone else to believe that He was <u>not</u> God. Because once your faith in Him as a man and ordinary like Shakespeare or Mahomet is sure and certain, once you really believe that He was <u>not</u> God, a host of difficulties arise. You are forced to find some explanation in order to account for the rise and growth and existence of the Church.

Renan's explanation is in a lesser degree that of G.B.S., that Our Lord was a madman. (To me it is far easier, taking all into consideration, to believe that He was God rather than a madman.) George Moore's explanation is that He recovered after the crucifixion.[2] This is to me incredible, i.e. more incredible than to believe He was God. And so on.

But if you believe that He was God, that He did found a Church, that that Church exists, unbroken in tradition and teaching since His death, everything becomes simple and among other things all the different versions of Our Lord's character.

For if He was God then G.B.S. is perfectly right in recognising in Him a partial portrait of himself and so is every man who ever lived, for every man is made in the image of God, however debased the portrait becomes. And I think G.B.S. quite right in finding fault with you for denying him his stamp of origin and superscription. And this applies to everyone else, Renan, G. Moore, Bombardier Wells,[3] and Lord Claud Hamilton.[4]

That is why to a <u>Catholic</u> there is nothing in the least blasphemous in G.B.S.'s remarks. As a priest in some book says to someone, 'Don't bother about what Protestants call blasphemous. They don't know what blasphemy means.'

G.B.S. when he talks of Christianity means Protestantism and admits as much. And when Protestants say they cannot manage the acrobatic feat of reconciling the Catholic Church with Christianity, what they really mean is that they cannot reconcile the Protestant conception of the Catholic Church with the Protestant conception of Christianity.

Yrs, M.B.

1 The *New Witness* was a magazine first edited by Belloc, then by Cecil Chesterton until he joined the Army, and finally by G. K. Chesterton. MacCarthy's article had appeared the previous day. Shaw had suggested in the *New Statesman* that it should be called 'The Three Witnesses' and that they should print an article on how they would deal with Jo – the poor boy in *Bleak House*. On 25 May G. K. Chesterton published an article 'Bernard Shaw and the Three Witnesses' which was followed by a further article on 1 June, and others joined in. MacCarthy's article discussed Shaw's preface to *Androcles and the Lion*, entitled by Shaw 'On the Prospects of Christianity'.

2 George Moore (1852–1933), Irish novelist and essayist, published his novel *The Brook Kerith*, based on the life of Christ, later this year, but M.B. was evidently already familiar with his arguments.

3 Bombardier Billy Wells (1888–1967), British heavyweight boxing champion 1911–19.

4 Lord Claud Hamilton (b. 1889), then a captain in the Grenadiers, had won the D.S.O. in 1914. M.B. is of course only rounding off the spectrum of society in citing him with Bombardier Wells, but whereas Wells became known for striking gongs (on screen, introducing films by J. Arthur Rank), Hamilton became quite practised at wearing them, filling several royal positions after his first appointment as Equerry-in-Ordinary to the Prince of Wales.

HILAIRE BELLOC Head Quarters, Royal Flying Corps, B.E.F.,
France
28.7.16

My dear H.,

Did you see Wells's article in the *Daily News* about Haynes and incidentally about the *New Witness* and you? It annoys me that people should take for granted that you and the *New Witness* are one and the same thing. Because although Cecil[1] means well, and although there is a great deal of truth at the bottom of what he means to present, he presents it in such a fashion that almost anyone who reads the *New Witness* for a spell either flies into a passion of rage or freezes into contempt. He has no judgement. Cecil, I mean, and he ruins a case by insisting on some irrelevant detail.

What annoys me most is that some people treat the *New Witness* as the official utterance of Catholic England and I can imagine people saying when they read some of the reckless statements and wildly intemperate and intolerant diatribes, 'If this is Catholicism give me Protestantism, Nonconformity or anything else.' Anyone who reads the *New Witness* for any length of time feels the same unless they take the whole thing as a joke. ... Also one gets tired of the tone. The kind of bullying shriek.

Write to me.

Yrs, M.B.

1 Cecil Edward Chesterton (1879–1918), G. K. Chesterton's brother. He joined the Highland Light Infantry and was killed. Journalist and editor of the *New Witness*. When he enlisted in the Army in October 1916 G. K. Chesterton took over the editorship as a duty.

JOHN SQUIRE   Advanced Head Quarters, Royal Flying Corps,
B.E.F., France
21.8.16

Dear Mr. Squire,

Even when it is not practically in one's bedroom there is nothing so noisy as an engine being tested. I wonder if they are rotary or stationary. I wonder if they are 160 Beardmores or 220 Rolls-Royces; and if rotary whether they are Rhônes or Monosoupape Gnomes, the latter I think the noisiest of any.

It is impossible to tie Desmond [MacCarthy]. He is illusive as thistledown. The only way to get him to write is to make sure he ought to have some other very pressing business to do. I haven't heard from him for weeks and months and he owes me many letters. But for all I know he may be a second-class air-mechanic or perhaps an acetylene welder in this Corps. It is full – the Corps I mean – of poets, musicians, organbuilders, jewellers, tailors, gaolers, goalers, goalkeepers, lawyers, bankers, solicitors, farmers, composers, tinkers and photographers.

... I have a great deal more to say on the subject of music-hall songs and songs. I have said most of it [in] print a long time ago. Briefly my experience is this, that the real beautiful native folk song ... only flourishes in countries where a lot of people are still illiterate, like Russia, Servia, Bulgaria, and that as soon as such people become educated, or semi-educated rather, what they eventually go for and love is mauk in music, songs like the 'Rosary', 'Thora' and the adventures of repentant prostitutes who die in slums after leaving the palaces of the rich.

Now in England, and in England alone, there is a counterblast to this mauk (and nowhere does the mauk reach to such an acute point as in England and nowhere is it so much wallowed in...). There is a counterblast I say... in the shape of the natural talent of the English for rhythm combined with *vis comica*, the *vis comica* being almost entirely the result of the rhythm, that is why the words themselves you quote, and I quote, and all your correspondents quote, are so rarely funny. But the combination is often irresistible. You hear the tune and you can't get it out of your head and you can't get the words out of your head.

I quite admit you don't often get the real stuff in the music halls, which only give a reflection of it, but you get it from the quarries out of which music hall artistes are made. You get it at soldiers' smoking concerts and sailors' singsongs. You get it sometimes in provincial music-halls and often in pantomimes.

One song I can think of which used to be popular:

> Book in any old time,
> Make yourself at home,
> Put your feet on the mantle shelf,
> Open the cupboard and help yourself.

In that last line the music rises with a peculiar lift and swings in a way which only an English tune can rise and swing.

'Tipperary', by the way, was an unsuccessful music-hall song made popular at a pantomime. I think it is one of the most beautiful tunes ever written. Of course the soldiers are sick of it and never sing it now. But it will always be the song of 1914. Just as the 'Marseillaise' was the song of '89 or was it '91? I forget.

To go back to my point, take a Russian soldier or sailor who will sing to you reams of what is probably the most beautiful folksong in the world with the most beautiful words. Introduce him to a song about something mawkish to a catchy sentimental tune and he will fly to it. That is why Archer need never expect to make old songs popular, or at least if he does expect to he will be disappointed.[1]

When I saw your second article the other day I was ashamed of myself for having added to your correspondence, so when I got your letter just now I was doubly pleased.

Among the French books, did you mention a little gem called *La Guerre Madame*?[2] I see that at last the works of O. Henry have been published in England.[3] About those you would find I think plenty to write. I have never been able to understand why they have not been published years ago. I was introduced to them by the Sub-Purser on board what is it called, a liner I suppose, not a thing like the *Lusitania* and not a thing like a P. & O., but a steamer that goes to Australia.[4]

... I cannot tell you what a great joy it is to get a letter and such a letter! You see all one's friends are either too busy or too sad or too proud to write.

Yours, M.B.

I have just learnt the MORSE ALPHABET.

1 William Archer (1856–1924), dramatic critic and editor of Ibsen, had attacked

in an article in *The Fortnightly* (August 1916, p. 253) the music-hall and music-hall songs, suggesting they had killed a genuine vein of lyrical faculty in the English people. Squire had defended music-hall songs in the *New Statesman* of 5 August. As a result he was overwhelmed with correspondence.

2 By Paul Géraldy, illustrated by Bernard Naudin. M.B.'s copy, given by the illustrator to the author and by the author to M.B., was sold at Sotheby's on 30 May 1961.

3 Pen name of William Sydney Porter (1862–1910), American short story writer.

4 See *Round the World in Any Number of Days.*

EDWARD MARSH   H.Q., R.F.C., B.E.F., France
                                    18 September 1916

My dear Eddy,

[A report] yesterday that Raymond [Asquith] has been killed.¹ I suppose there is not the faintest chance of its not being true. I had dinner with him when he passed through Montreuil on his way to join his regiment and I had a chill foreboding, amounting almost to certainty, that I should never see him again. All our friends of every generation appear to be doomed. There is no one we shall miss more than Raymond. ... But how far finer his fate is than if he had ended up with a successful career at the Bar. This event crowds out everything else to me and I feel it difficult to write about anything else or to think of anything else.

I cannot cope with the Dostoievsky book at present.² ... I believe Dostoievsky is one of the most untranslatable of writers. One somehow takes for granted he wrote badly because of a certain hurry and form-lessness till one suddenly realizes that his spoken word, his dialogue, his soliloquy, his analysis is almost <u>transcendently</u> written. Everyone discovered this when scenes of *The Brothers Karamazov* were acted at Moscow. It was found impossible to transpose a comma. He writes badly, then, in the sense that Shakespeare writes badly, compared with Congreve. ...

Yours, M.

P.S. I think George Moore's book [*The Brook Kerith*] is exactly like every other effort made at rewriting the Gospels ... All these people do not seem to understand that the great point of the Gospels – looked upon merely as a story, as an 'ordinary book', as the undergraduate said to Jowett ('Really, Mr. Jones, you must think it a very <u>extraordinary</u> book') – is its terseness and that it is as striking by what is left out as by what is put in. George Moore tells the story of 'To Caesar thou hast appealed, to Caesar shalt thou go', and adds the words '<u>by the next ship</u>'. That would be enough to spoil everything but '*non content*' with this, he adds a page-long sentence. It is as if you took a speech in Shakespeare, 'To Mantua go', and added 'at the earliest possible opportunity, by the next post-chaise, and don't forget your luggage'.

M.B.

1 He had been killed in action on the Somme on 15 September.
2 *Fyodor Dostoevsky. A Critical Study* by J. Middleton Murry.

H. G. WELLS   H.Q., R.F.C., B.E.F., France
22.9.16

My dear H. G.,

I have finished your book [*Mr Britling Sees It Through*] ... I think the picture of the pre-war mood is amazing, and doubtless that of England during the beginning of the war is equally good – all that is a closed book to me. The part which deals with the war ... is very good also but there fiction has to compete with such a lot of fact that fiction <u>now</u> is handicapped. It won't be in twenty years' time. ... I see now that in war – and all wars are essentially alike – a great deal of muddle happens which is due not necessarily to any incompetence, want of organisation or education or military knowledge, but simply to the destructive potentialities of war and to chance. For instance (this is an imaginary case) you order a gas attack at 4 p.m. on a certain Tuesday if the wind is right. The wind <u>is</u> right. At 3 p.m. the wind changes. Someone notices the change and telephones to those whom it concerns to put off the attack. A shell breaks the telephone – the attack is not put off and this is put down to bad staff work. You see?

When I was in Manchuria I saw lots of things happen which seemed incredible. I put it down to the Slav temperament. In this war I saw all these same things happen in the same way, and heard people attribute it to the English want of training and organisation. But then from wireless messages and prisoners' accounts I saw the same things happen to the

Germans! Of course I'm not saying there haven't often been mistakes and bad mistakes made owing to bad training, staff work etc., but far more often these things were the result of circumstances over which no one had any control.

Troops arrive too late. People say, why wasn't this foreseen? It was foreseen and the troops had been sent hours <u>earlier</u> than they had been asked for, but something else happened, something to the roads, or other troops in some other place lost their officers, took the wrong road, blocked the road. I am giving an imaginary instance. I remember in the retreat frantic messages in the wireless ... testifying to utter muddle and dislocation. This was not due to plans not having been made but [to] plans having been <u>upset</u>, <u>dislocated</u>. Again, in attacks, and sometimes in successful attacks, officers are killed, NCOs are killed, and men are left with gaping eyes wondering what to do next.

One fact people don't realize is that our army, for its size, was about the best trained army in the world. Another thing they don't realize is that certain things have happened which were sheer triumphs of organisation. The management of the transport in the retreat for instance, and still more the getting away of the army from the Dardanelles. We hear of all the failures. The successes are not mentioned. I could cite you many cases in point in our army and the French of instances of either kind, of success and of failure. Another train of thought your book has started in me. The Germans: the things their newspapers say: they go on and on in exactly the same way as they did before the war, they seem to have <u>learnt nothing</u> and <u>forgotten nothing</u>. Have you ever read a German text history book prepared for schools, a 'History of the World' for German youth, and noticed the part England is made to play? If not, do. It is highly instructive. Have you ever read *The History of Philosophy in Germany in the 19th Century* by Heine? It has nothing to do with philosophy but is highly illuminating and brilliant. All this is to say that your book is like a dazzling tonic.

I rather hope you won't confine yourself to books about sheer <u>actuality</u> because after all one is not in perspective, and to <u>see</u> a thing you must look back at it. But I am very glad you wrote *Mr Britling Sees It Through*.

Yrs, Maurice

HILAIRE BELLOC   H.Q., R.F.C.
                                                  24.9.1916
My dear H.,

... Evan [Charteris] wrote to me and told me that you had (a) beaten
him at chess, (b) exasperated him by talking of the Catholic Church,
which he says to you is but a social system which poisons relations in
every walk of life, i.e. the fact of it being a system poisons etc.

Take my advice. Never never never talk theology or discuss the
Church with those outside it. It is not a subject which can be discussed
from the outside. People simply don't understand what one is talking
about and they merely (a) get angry, (b) come to the conclusion one does-
n't believe in the thing oneself and that one is simply doing it to annoy.

This is tiresome because it is really such an interesting topic, but I
think God evidently intends everybody to find his way on these roads
entirely unaided. This is why conversations about the Church between
a Cat' and a Prot' merely lead to bad blood and to a total misunder-
standing.

Evan says that you have killed all the sympathy he had for the eccle-
sia and I think that is probably a good thing, as it was probably the
wrong sort of sympathy.

Write to me at your leisure but write to me at length.
                                        Yours affec., O. Maur.

G. K. CHESTERTON   H.Q., R.F.C., B.E.F., France
                                          29.9.16
My dear Gilbert,

I have just been reading the Grenfell book which is I think like a
Constable with Sir Joshua figures walking about in the trees.[1] I should
like foreigners to read it and to say to them this is what we are fighting
for and these are the radiant beings we sacrificed gladly to keep our
heritage of trees and fields. ...

Death has been terribly busy lately among my friends. Mr. Cornish
whom I loved dearly and to whom I owe all the poor (opposite of)
Kultur that I possess. Raymond Asquith. There was no waste there. His
death was trebly glorious from his not being a regular soldier, from his
having refused to remain in a safe billet such as I am in now and have
always been in during this war. But the eclipse for his wife is tragic.

Beside this, many of my new friends have been killed and my old aunt Lady Ponsonby, a lady of infinite wit, wisdom, tradition and Englishness (unlike her son Arthur but like her son John, who is the best loved General in the British Army), is dying.

Gilbert, one feels very inglorious being on a staff. In the Manchurian campaign, after I had at the beginning of the war a week's experience of living with a staff (and that was a Brigade staff where I lived in extreme discomfort), I vowed that, come what might, I would get away from it and never do such a thing again. I escaped and attached myself to a battery.

But it so turned out in this war that without knowing what I was doing I got nailed to a staff, but had it not been so I could not have come out at the beginning of the war. And at that time no one foresaw anything. As it is I like my work[2] and I believe I really am of some use to the General who I am working with, who is a great man with a spirit of flame. His name is General Trenchard. He says he is descended from Jack Sheppard[3] and I can well believe it. He has the energy in overcoming obstacles, the initiative, the swift decision, the foresight and intuition of that illustrious prison breaker.

I make all his notes. And they are many, for he has the eye of an eagle. And he thinks far too quickly to write.

Still, compared to what the others are all doing, it is very inglorious and safe. But then I ought to be thankful to be here at all. I like my work and (Oh Inconsistency!) I wouldn't be elsewhere for worlds. ... I know one thing: that this is the only time in my life when I have been of the slightest use to anyone. Also I think I cheer the pilots up...

Yrs, M.B.

1 *Pages from a Family Journal* by Lady Desborough.
2 He was engaged in drafting a summary of the basic principles of air strategy which are still valid. Boyle, p. 186.
3 (1702–24), the Stepney cat burglar, hanged at Tyburn.

H. G. WELLS   H.Q., R.F.C., B.E.F, France
                                                              4.10.16

And in scribbling all that I did scribble to you, my dear H.G., impertinently enough, about *Mr Britling*, I forgot to tell you the main thought that it left me with, and this was – what do you think – the thought of

<u>Ireland</u>! I think it ought to be the most urgent, pressing and imperative duty of all people who have, like you, the power of influence by the pen, to do all you possibly can to lead English public opinion, to <u>force</u> English Government, whatever it is then, to solve the Irish question by admitting at last, and once and for all, that there is an Irish nation, but alas! as I write the words I know it is more complicated than that. The bitter seeds were sown long ago. Recently too, and we have to reap the harvest.

One can't take a sponge and say all that doesn't count. Nor can one take a mop and a scrubbing brush, as you so often urge, and tidy up the mess, the mess of crime that is born of stupidity and stubbornness, and kindness and prejudice. Nevertheless I hope. It seems so unutterably silly when one thinks of it. But then man is a silly animal struggling in a mist.

Yours, M.B.

HILAIRE BELLOC [France]

4.10.16

My Dear Hil.,

I should like you to go into Parliament again for many reasons. I should like all people of any intelligence and usefulness, as soon as the war is over, to do everything in their power to bring everyone to their senses about Ireland. A cynic would say, 'Including the Irish themselves'. But whatever the Irish are to blame for they didn't begin it. It's not a question of *Que messieurs les assassins commencent.* We were the *messieurs les assassins qui commencaient.* I admit they were to blame in this last and saddest of revolutions but what was that but the seeds of our own old follies and the crimes we did years ago. The seeds are sown and one has to put up with the harvest, come it never so late. I wish they hadn't shot any of the rebels ... I daresay they deserved it. But I wish that our Government had said, 'Whatever killing has been done there shall be no <u>more</u> now.' ... I hope in spite of all that if you ever get into Parliament one of your duties must be to try to convince and persuade people that they must recognize the fact that Ireland is a nation. Of course I know there is one great difficulty, namely that the Irish will probably oppose an Irish Government as much as any other. (They sympathize with Carson[1] because he was anti-Government.) But still there is a lot to be tried. The growing prosperity of the country will, I hope, help things. But how silly it all seems. ...

Yrs, M.

1 Edward Henry Carson (1854–1935), Irish barrister, judge and Unionist politician. Kt. 1900. Lord of Appeal in Ordinary 1921–9.

LADY JULIET DUFF   H.Q., R.F.C., B.E.F., France
26.1.17

Chère Pêche Melba,

A tragedy of far-reaching import happened today. Yesterday we started on a tour of a Brigade including kite balloons, and incidentally we slept in the coldest house I have ever endured. The water froze while one waited. There was central heating and hotwater pipes but there was no coal, and the pipes had burst in the frost, being full of cold water. The floors and staircase were made of solid stone. The doors of glass and the windows of fine old cracked glass. The bedrooms, which had no fireplaces, had not been lived in since the twelfth century and then only by serfs. There was no coal in the house and a very little thin firewood such as is used by housemaids to lay a fire with. The house stood on the banks of a frozen river, in point of fact the Somme. On the other side of the house was a marsh. The ground was covered with frozen snow. The wind cut like a razor. The thermometer registered 14 degrees of frost centigrade and 47 degrees according to something else.

Nevertheless I enjoyed the outing. And by drinking enough boiling whisky before going to bed, I was sufficiently unconscious to lose sight of the cold. The next day we spent looking at balloons. On our way back – and this is the tragedy – our luggage fell off the Rolls Royce, the General's suitcase made of Willesden canvas, containing his razor, his new coat, his trousers, his shoes, his favourite buttonhook, and an advance copy of the *News of the World*, and my little *entout cas*, bought in St. Petersburg, which has been round the world and all over the Balkans, twice to Constantinople, and through the length and breadth of Russia and the Central Empires. Messengers have been despatched to look for it and I have hopes of its being found as I have invoked St. Anthony who has never failed me yet. ...

Your loving Pair et Impair. Rouge couleur.

[118]

EDMUND GOSSE   H.Q., R.F.C., B.E.F., France
                                                              12.4.17

My dear Carissimo Maestro,

   Your *Swinburne* arrived last night and I finished it early this morning before I got up.[1] I only wished for more. I will tell you all the little
things that occurred to me as I read. ... In discussing 'Songs Before Sun-
rise' I wonder you didn't comment on 'Super Flumina Babylonis'. That
has always seemed to me to touch the high water mark of Swinburne's
genius ... I think this poem influenced Claudel in his great *Ode on the
War*. Swinburne's great influence on Gabriele D'Annunzio is an interesting point ... I rather wonder you said nothing about the direct influence of the Old Testament on Swinburne's early verse. ... he is saturated
with the diction of the Old Testament. This influence seen through his
temperament and his art is very traceable, I think, in Kipling's early
verse... Once when I was playing a game of giving one line of poetry by
itself and the author had to be guessed, I gave the line 'Blow all one way
to shelter it', and Eddy Marsh said Swinburne at once. We both thought
it remarkable how a poet can so unmistakably imprint his personality
on six monosyllables and one two-syllable word. Chesterton calls attention to Swinburne's use of monsyllables like 'short Roman swords'. ...
                                                  Yrs, M.B.

1 *The Life of Algernon Charles Swinburne* (1917). M.B. wrote to Marsh on the
same day: 'I have just finished Gosse's *Swinburne*. I enjoyed it very much and
wish it were more indiscreet and less impersonal and less modest. Even aerated
waters are not mentioned. And some of the supreme touches are left out of the
story... I think he had not thought enough of posterity and too much of his
contemporaries...' For the reply to this see Charteris pp. 410–11. Gosse included
amongst the difficulties he suffered: '1 The extraordinary hostility of the family.
2 The embargo laid on any mention of drunkenness. 3 A still heavier sexual
embargo...'

DESMOND MACCARTHY   H.Q., R.F.C, B.E.F., France
                                                              14.4.17

Dear Desmond,

   Your article about H. G. is frightfully good.[1] A masterpiece of discre-
tion...

   Do you know what I think is at the bottom of the case of H. G.
Wells? Harmsworthia. War hysteria with a touch of megalomania. The

something-must-be-done attitude, followed by suggesting something quasi-insane. Do you remember his letter to *The Times* at the beginning of the war?[2] Harmsworthlike he catches on to the last phase in the air and shrilly advocates it. Of course he is perfectly sincere and it is not his fault that he is half-baked outside his genius.

In his latest book, which I think is really less silly than the preceding one, his Theology is really Greek isn't it? A God of courage (Ares or Apollo), a God of youth (Hermes), a rebellious, finite, suffering God, working for and with humanity, but helpless (Prometheus), and in the background a veiled figure, Zeus or Kronos or Demogorgon. That veiled figure always has to be invented. So it comes to this, I believe in two Gods but not in one person. One finite and the other undefined.

His remarks on the Councils and the dogma of the Trinity betray not only ignorance but a complete unfamiliarity with the subject, the same ignorance that Herbert Spencer would have been led to betray had he dined with staff of the *Sporting Times* at Romano's and racing matters had been discussed.

I should like to hear from you very much. Is there the slightest chance of it?

It is hot, thundery, and I have got a headache.

Yrs, M.B.

1 'Religion and Mr. Wells', a review of Wells's book *God the Invisible King* had appeared in the *New Statesman* on 12 May.
2 The letter, 8 August 1914, headed 'The Use of the Untrained', advocated the formation of something like what was to be the Home Guard in the Second World War.

HILAIRE BELLOC [France]

14.7.17

... Did you see Arnold Bennett's sentence about Gilbert [Chesterton] in which he said that anyone who accepted dogma <u>at this time of day</u> had an inferior intellectual <u>apparatus</u>? I thought this very funny. I wonder if he thinks he has on the whole a more powerful [mind] than St. Thomas Aquinas, Lord Acton and Duchesne. That is the whole essence of half-bakedness and semi-Kultur ...

For Belloc's reply to this see Speaight, Letter 86.

H.Q., R.F.C., B.E.F., France
                                                      20.8.17

Dear Sir,

It is now 3.15 p.m. I have just this moment finished reading a book called *The Loom of Youth*. I began it the night before last, read it far into the night, forced myself to stop, took it up again last night, again forced myself to stop, took it up this morning and in spite of interruptions, went on and finished it. I should like it to have been twice as long.

I saw it reviewed by Squire and I asked him to send it me if he had finished with it and he did. He said in his review that the school was easily recognisable. I daresay it is but I don't know which school it represents.[1] All my knowledge of schools except of the one I was at is derived from books and of those books the only lifelike one I have read is *The Harrovians*.[2]

I was at Eton myself and the worship of athletics was as great there, as much a religion and a matter of course as what you describe. I was myself no good at games and never got a single colour. Nor was I much good at work, nor did I try to be, but while I was at school I never wished the circumstances to be different. Perhaps if I had been a brilliantly successful athlete I should have done so (no, I certainly shouldn't have then), as it was I was grateful ... grateful that the prevalent religion and everyone's engrossment in it allowed one to do what one liked in one's corner.

My corner was in the Boys' Library and on the river and there undisturbed I discovered English literature for myself. I felt unconsciously (of course I did not formulate it thus) like Renan when he said that if so many thousand people didn't frequent race meetings, it would be impossible for him to study Hebrew in his top floor, or words to that effect.

After I left Eton I went for a time to a school in Germany and later, after Universities and exams, I travelled a lot all over Europe and in Russia and saw something of the education there as well as that of other continental countries. At first for a long time after I had grown up I was an ardent champion for public school educational reform and even now I think every word you say in your book on this question is true, but I believe there is another side. I don't feel now so very ardent a champion of absolute change. That is to say, reform, electrify, vivify, but be careful what you put in place of the old and take care that the new system be not worse than the old.

[121]

I don't suppose that education can ever be really very good. I mean the sensible, <u>live</u>, stimulating masters must always be exceptions and I can imagine that a modern system could become just as tiresome and conventional as the most conventional classics and cricket system. Imagine a Nietzsche class led by Rogers. People seem to me now in the same breath to be denouncing the results of <u>Kultur</u> and to be advocating the adoption of the causes of the very results we are fighting to destroy. … Take, again, the Russian system of education where culture, all-round culture, is made as much a fetish as football at your school and mine. I think the results of it are depressing to a degree. A man is ashamed if he doesn't know the name of D'Annunzio's latest book, the latest piece of music in all countries, the last draughtsman. A hallmark is set up and if you haven't got that hallmark you are an outcast. Atheism is a matter of course and a certain half-baked philosophy … and all sorts of shibboleths. But all this is remote from real <u>culture</u>, as remote as <u>Kultur</u> is, so I come to the conclusion that true education is within, like the Kingdom of Heaven, and can only be sought and obtained by the individual himself and in spite of the official education whether that be ancient or modern. I of course quite agree that as far as possible boys should be given the opportunity of learning what interests them and not be forced to learn only the things that could never interest them.

What I think about the games question is not that the athleticism is bad but the professional element that is introduced into games spoils everything. There didn't seem to be as much of that at your school in the football at least … nor was there in Eton football, but it had crept into the cricket while I was there and in the way games were directed and looked upon by the masters. I think professionalism is the death of all games and the reason why I like some aspects of the educational side of our public schools is that it is so frankly amateurish. However you will probably think all this bosh. In any case I have thought over these things for years and certainly gone through what some of the characters in your book went through, on a minor, humbler scale. I suppose boys are more precocious now. Collectively I mean. Certain things are in the air which everyone imbibes. For instance I only discovered *Atalanta in Calydon* the last year I was at school. I left at seventeen. *Poems and Ballads* not till after I had left.[3] But I discovered nearly all the rest of English poetry at school.

I apologize for this long rambling letter. You may like to know that you had at least one attentive and absorbed reader who thought your book all too short and was amazed at its performance ... and who looks forward with certainty to further and still greater achievements from its author.

Yours sincerely,

M. Baring, Major R.F.C

1 The book was based on Sherborne. Rogers was a schoolmaster caricatured in it.
2 By Arnold Lunn (1913).
3 Swinburne.

LYTTON STRACHEY   H.Q., Independent Force, R.A.F., B.E.F.,

France

June 10, 1918

Dear Mr Strachey,

My excuse for writing to you is that we once met at the Lyttons;[1] and I have read and greatly admired your book on French literature and other writings... I have just read your brilliant *Eminent Victorians* and I cannot help writing at once to tell you that I think your portrait of my uncle Evelyn Baring is unfair and untrue to life in every respect.[2]

Of course you have a perfect right to draw his portrait as it leaps to your mind from his works which are, I suppose, your only sources of information, but may I supplement these sources by a few personal reminiscences? I think a nephew is about the most impartial judge an uncle can have. How prone a nephew is to see the faults of an uncle! You say he was a reticent, cautious diplomat with a diplomat's training and a 'diplomat's conscience', that he rarely said what he thought, that he hated the East, looked forward to a country place and being an 'institution'. I contest every word of this.

1 He did not have a diplomat's training. He was the non-favourite son of a large family, considered as a boy the ugly duckling and black sheep and sent to Woolwich to be a gunner. NB Not to Eton or any public school but a sort of Squeers private school where flogging and strong nasty medicine never broke his dogged obstinacy.[3] After that he became a gunner but he never entered the Diplomatic Service and it was chance sent him to Egypt. For data on what he was like as an ADC in the Ionian Islands, apply to Father Bowden at the Oratory, a fellow

[123]

ADC. He had an active mind, vehemently and passionately curious. He was <u>not</u> brought up on the classics. He never 'kept up' his classics but hurled himself with characteristic vigour into the study of them comparatively late. He learnt French after he was 30, [ancient] Greek through modern Greek, and Turkish much later.

2 I should have thought that all who knew him would agree that his main characteristic was an outspokenness and directness and bluntness of speech amounting sometimes to brutality. His chief fault I should have said was his ungovernable abruptness. His desire to get straight to the point.

3 All the account of the Gordon negotiations in his book is, I think, slightly bowdlerized. I mean I regret he did not publish all the things he wrote. I know he didn't want to give unnecessary pain to Lord Granville's relations.

4 You talk of his reading Gordon's telegrams with a sub-acid smile! You may get that impression from his book but throw yourself back into his place, with Gordon absolutely lost and Hanning [Speke] reading Isaiah in the desert and Granville variable, witty, vacillating and always urbane at the FO and Mr G[ladstone]. not caring a button about foreign affairs.[4] I am old enough to remember the echoes of his voice and the accounts of his days and nights of agony and bloody sweat. His 'razor edge' policy was generally based on getting at what Gordon really meant and wanted and that is why he kept the telegrams, to be able to piece together something coherent out of the contradictions of the 12 hours. Because as he said, if you got *at* what Gordon *really* meant, it was often right.

5 He took no interest in the East. This is untrue. I have heard him talk of Eastern things by the hour. He had endless note books full of such things concerning Eastern habits and the differences between Eastern ways of thought and ours. He learnt Turkish. His secretary Boyle was a great Arabic scholar. He never could get used to cold English summers to the end of his life.

6 If he ever dreamt of a country place (which I'm sure he didn't), he never got it. He lived at Wimpole Street and died there.

7 If he wanted to be an institution, he thrice refused posts which would have made him far more of an institution. He refused one so as not to be far from his children.

8 He was passionately fond of many kinds of literature. Vide his

commonplace books and printed vols., his articles in *Spectator* 2 vols., Ed. Gosse's article on him.

9 When you got over his initial abruptness he was a delightful talker and especially kind to the young, always ready to take an interest in anything.

10 It is true he had many violent dislikes, including the prose of Walter Pater and the verse of Browning, but he liked Homer, Theocritus, the [Greek] Anthology and modern Greek prose. His library is of immense interest and his historical knowledge wide and miscellaneous and varied to a degree.

11 He was a keen student of foreign nations, all nations ... and made very shrewd remarks about Germans, Austrians, Prussians, Italians.

12 Gordon was right, I think, to say that Granville was the chief factor... You say [Cromer] was a nonentity, but, French scholar as you are, I think his French would have put you to shame. He is the only Englishman I have ever heard of who made with triumphant success a witty speech in French to a French audience and that audience the Comédie Française of 1870, which included Delaunay, Coquelin, Sarah Bernhardt, Monet, Sully and Maubant.

Of course your portrait of C. as the typical official and diplomat ... , Gordon as a symphony in grey and steel, makes your Essay more artistic. It heightens the irony but I think you have unconsciously sacrificed truth (here) to art.

He certainly had the courage of his opinions and had he been in the position of Pontius Pilate I am convinced he would have done everything except shelve the responsibility and wash his hands.

The populace at Cairo (better judges than you or I) had an ineradicable and profound belief in his justice. His motive – his only motive in Egypt – was to do his duty and the best for the country in circumstances of overwhelming difficulty and crushing anxiety. You might have in fairness quoted his words when he finally accepted Gordon's appointment and where he admits to the full that he made and that he knew at the time he was making a tragic mistake ...[5]

Yours sincerely,
Maurice Baring

1 The 2nd Earl and Countess of Lytton were friends of M.B.
2 (1841–1917), 1st Earl of Cromer, author of *Modern Egypt*.

3 Ordnance School, Carshalton.
4 In 1868 Granville became colonial secretary in Gladstone's first ministry, and in 1870 foreign secretary; then foreign secretary again 1880–85.
5 As consul-general in Egypt, he had reluctantly consented to Gordon's mission to the Sudan in 1884.

Note. In a letter to Belloc of 9 June 1918, commenting on the same book, MB wrote: 'The things intelligent Protestants write about Catholics – and he is very intelligent and writes extremely well – fill me with wonder and amazement. ... Read his article on Manning and you will see. ... It never occurs to these people that Catholics may possibly believe the Catholic faith to be true. Which would of course explain a great deal. They regard this explanation as one to be ruled out of court.' And in a letter to Lady Desborough, written the following day, he wrote: 'It is brilliant and extremely well written but I do not like it. To me it gives the impression of a rather small and fundamentally inhuman [man], dissecting with extreme skill but with a rather bitter bias, men very much greater than himself.'

WILLIAM ORPEN   R.F.C., H.Q.
                                                        June 1918

> Dear Woppy I am glad that you
> Will soon be back at G.H.Q.
> With brushes, paint and turpentine,
> And canvases fourteen by nine,
> To paint the British soldier man
> As often as you may and can.
> The brave ally, the captive Boche,
> And Monseur Clemenceau and Foch;
> But, on the whole, you'd better not
> Paint lady spies before they're shot.
> We're living in the Eastern Zone,
> Between the ——, the ——, the ——
> (The orders of Sir Douglas Haig
> Compel me, Woppy, to be vague.)
> But you can find out where we are
> And come there in a motor-car.
> We hold a château on a hill
> ————————————— (censored)
> A pond with carp, a stream with brill,
> And perch and trout await your skill.

A garden with umbrageous trees
Is here for you to take your ease.
And strawberries, both red and white,
Are there to soothe your appetite;
And, just the very thing for you,
Sweet landscape and a lovely view.
So pack your box and come along
And take a ticket for Boulogne.
The general is calling me.
Yours, till we meet again,

M.B.

LYTTON STRACHEY   HQ Independent Force, R.A.F., B.E.F., France
July 17, 1918

Dear Mr. Strachey,

I have been reading the various letters which your book has elicited in various periodicals and as I have myself taken part in the correspondence I want to make one or two things quite clear. I dare say it is hardly necessary. I dare say you will have realized what I am going to say already.

Firstly I want to say that *I* do not think you are an iconoclast. I think your process of gently washing off the whitewash leaves your subjects greater than they were before, whenever you turn your imaginative insight on to them. That is to say in the case of Gordon and Miss Nightingale.

But sometimes you seem to me to turn your antipathy rather than your sympathy on to your subjects and the result, although amusing, leaves one sceptical as to the reality of the portrait.

(With your system you have no right to do this. You ought to do what Browning does in *The Ring and the Book*.)

I am not talking of Cromer. I am thinking of Arnold. I am thinking of Manning. Your essay doesn't account for Arnold though every word of it may be true. If that *was* all, there would have been no Arnold influence.

I was amused by the review in the *Spectator*. They scold you for your Cromer and your Clough (was it Clough?) because they approve of Cromer and Clough. But they commend you for your Manning because

[127]

they disapprove of Manning. Personally I feel your Manning essay doesn't account at all for Manning.

A minor point about Cromer in the East. You say it is grotesque to imply you didn't and don't realize Cromer's knowledge and interest in Eastern administrative methods etc. but that you meant that C. was like a man with great knowledge of counterpoint but no feeling for music. But what you <u>say</u> is this: 'His life's work had an element of paradox in it. It was passed … in the East and the East meant very little to him: <u>he took no interest in it</u>. It was a thing to be looked after. It was also a convenient field for the talents of Sir Evelyn Baring.'

Well, anyone reading that would be bound to have I think the idea that he was the kind of the not uncommon type of Englishman who spends his whole life in a foreign country without realising that the people around him are different than they are [here]. That they are human and strangely subtle and complex.

Now I leave all Cromer's administrative work to historians. It may have been good or bad, right or wrong, founded on misconception or founded on reality, that is the business of history: the documents and results are there. But what I do know and what I have a right to say from a personal point of view (as it is a thing that concerns the man's character as an individual) is that Cromer took an interest in the oriental as a human being and was interested, amused and fascinated by the workings of the oriental mind. You may say he got it all wrong. But if you say that you are making a pretty big claim unless you yourself have first hand knowledge of the East. But to me the interesting thing is that the orientals <u>understood him</u>: that is to say the Fellaheen did. You could see that from the way they talked to him in Cairo and right down the Nile. This I know from experience. The little differences he noted between orientals and occidentals were of a kind that only a mind which is interested and fascinated in the East, and only a mind which has a certain penetrative insight, can note at all.

To me he was the opposite of a man like Sidney Lee who writes a book showing you he knows more about Shakespeare lore [than anyone else] in the world and leaves you wondering whether he has the slightest notion of what the plays and the poems are really like.[1]

But this is [a] small point: your real injustice, I think, towards him is that you do not realize the anxiety of responsibility, the stress of the work, what it must have been like while it was going on, with a

Dostoievsky-like character at the other end in the desert. His surviving brother (have I told you this?) says the anxiety and the strain and the work at that time nearly killed him. You judge it ... from his own calm retrospect or from his calm official letters. It was a good thing they were calm.

But what I wrote this letter [for] was to say that I think, in spite of all, your system of biography is the right one, only I think you have sometimes abused the dangerously sharp weapon of irony that you possess. Irony used against big men leads, I think, to all sorts of misunderstandings. Lemaître says the same thing about Renan, *cela fatigue à la longue*.

Don't answer. And forgive me for writing what I have no doubt is an unneeded, importunate and impertinent letter.

Yrs sincerely,
Maurice Baring

1 Sidney Lee (1859–1926), Kt. 1911. Professor of English, editor *Dictionary of National Biography* 1891–1917. His *A Life of William Shakespeare* (1898) was for many years the standard work.

Note. These letters, with the damaging (and accurate) quotation from Strachey's book, produced a reply from Strachey. See Michael Holroyd, *Lytton Strachey, A Critical Biography*, vol. 2 (London, 1968), pp. 320–2.

AIR MARSHAL SIR HUGH TRENCHARD, K.C.B., D.S.O.

Brooks' Club
December 23, 1918

Dear General,

I have just found your letter here. It is better than any Christmas present and more precious than rubies. Of course all you say about me is absurd but it is very nice of you to say it all the same and it is very nice to hear it. Undeserved rewards, as someone once said, are exquisite.

Nothing will persuade me that your career is finished. But whatever shape it may take in the future I can only repeat what I said to you before, <u>that I am here</u> and should like to be with you wherever you go, whether it is Abyssinia or Farnborough or West Africa or East Ham, or the Colonial Office or the War Office ... or the Russian Coast.

I am self supporting. If nothing happens I can get along perfectly well but if it is a question of service, of public service, having served with the best, the second best – however good – is not good enough for me. There is a Latin proverb which says 'I see higher things and approve them; I carry out the lower'.[1] I am afraid I have done this all my life but I have seen the higher things and this has made me fastidious so that I seek for and demand the best literature and the best pictures (not mine!) and the best wine and the best cigars, failing that any – the worst – but not the second [best], but I feel this about people too.

If I am to admire a human being and not merely to like him I want quality of a high order, and if I am to think a man a great man he must be a real great man.

All my life I wanted to serve with and under such a man and my wish was gratified from 1915 to 1918. I can only pray that this precious privilege will not be taken away but may continue, unworthy as I know I am of it.

I will not re-read this letter as, if I did, I should probably tear it up ...

I wish you all the happiness and honour that you deserve. You have already got what is more precious than all acknowledgements, the complete devotion of a great number of men 'to the uttermost and to the last', of whom this most insignificant but not the least devoted is

Yrs, M.B.

1 *Video meliora proboque, deteriora sequor* (Ovid).

Note. A later letter, of 23 March 1920, explains that because of a severe illness MB was unable to accept Trenchard's invitation to return to work for him.

DAME ETHEL SMYTH   Brooks' Club
                                                  October 16, 1919

Beloved E.,

... It has always struck me, and did strike me before I was a Catholic, that the ideas non-Catholics have about the relations of Catholics to the priesthood are fantastic. When I was twenty I remember hearing a conversion (that of a young man I knew) discussed at a dinner. The following conversation took place:

A. 'Young so and so has become an R.C.'

B. 'What made him do that?'

A. 'Got hold of by the priests.'

B. (Satisfied) 'Of course. Got hold of by the priests.'

Now I knew that this man had never seen a priest (he was at Eton and Cambridge with me and was converted before leaving Cambridge) till the day he walked into the Brompton Oratory and stated his intention of becoming a Catholic. This was very much my case. I had never had a conversation on religion with a priest till I did the same.

That is one point.

Another is non-Catholics never realize how much Catholics dissociate the office and the man. The priest is a kind of *Bradshaw* ... Of course you can no doubt quote cases but it takes a lot to make a world and I think I am right in saying that the very devout, the most truly devout, Catholics are those who [see] priests almost exclusively sacramentally and not personally.

Laura [Lovat] says her mother-in-law, now a nun, never had personal relations with any priest. She didn't see anything of priests out of office hours so to speak. This is why when I read the sentence in your book about Catholics not being responsible ... I didn't know what it meant. ...

To me the difference between being a Catholic and being anything else is simply that if you are a Catholic you assume responsibility for all your acts, words and thoughts... You assume responsibility. The priest is merely the ticket office of the journey or the *bureau d'information*. In fact this fact is the explanation of why I ever became a Catholic. At one moment I came to the conclusion that human life is either casual or divine. If divine it meant a revealed representative. Where was this? The Catholic Church. And then everything follows down to the holy water. But if it is not divine, then the only alternative would be for me complete agnosticism. No third philosophy could satisfy me and no patent religion such as Xtian Science, Spiritualism, Theosophy, Table-turning. As for Buddhism, all oriental religions and Greek Philosophy, they seemed to me Prophecies of Christianity which found at last their full expression in Christianity, i.e. in Catholicism. Anglicanism seemed to me a lopped branch and ten years in Russia convinced me that the Orthodox Church (more attractive to me outwardly than R. C.dom) was not a lopped but a bent schismatic branch and suffered from that, i.e. instead of one Pope you had a million (State creeping in) and *tout ce qui s'ensuît*. So directly I came to the conclusion inside that life was for

[131]

me divine and that I had inside me an immortal thing in touch with an Eternal Spirit, there was no other course open to me than to become a Catholic. It took me 9 years from the day I had that conviction to reach the conclusion of my journey.

That in brief is the history of my religious experience! I don't know why I burden you with it. Yes I do. It is because I am very, very fond of you and I know you will understand. Also you have been through the same kind of thing. I once discussed it with H. B. [Brewster] after I had reached <u>Stage 1</u> and before I had reached <u>Stage B</u> and he told me he was all for people becoming Catholics if they thought like that, as long as they were actuated by such motives and not by outward things like candles and incense (all [of] which never did and never has affected me).

I can only add that I have never regretted it and that not only have I become convinced every day that it is true but I feel human life, which is almost intolerable as it is, would be to me quite <u>intolerable</u> without this belief, which is to me no narcotic but <u>food</u>, <u>air</u>, <u>drink</u>.

You said to me one day wouldn't you like to be a monk? Yes indeed, but I think it is like saying to a business man wouldn't you like to be a Rothschild. ...

God bless you, dearest Ethel,

Yrs, M.B.

DAME ETHEL SMYTH   Pickwick's Villa, Dulwich Village,
                                    London, S.E. 21
                                    October 24, 1919

Beloved E.,

... Of course, Ethel, if you can accept any religion which involves right and wrong mattering, then at once you assume responsibility. But I was thinking of my case and the point is I couldn't accept any of the [other] religions, i.e. Eastern religions, Anglicanism I absolutely disbelieved in; [it] was radically spoilt to me by its fundamental position, Greek Church.

Therefore the choice for me lay between R. Catholicism, which I could intellectually understand believing in before I did so myself, and what I call for lack of a better word Paganism. Paganism is, of course, a misnomer but I really mean materialism, with the belief of nothing really mattering. I heard of a priest saying years ago that there were only three things necessary to become a Catholic: 1. *Croire en Dieu*. 2. *Suivre sa conscience*. 3. *Aimer son prochain autant que soi même*. And I always felt that if I could accept these three *données* the whole of the rest followed.

My difficulty was to accept one and two.

I think the value of priests [is] that whatever their private lives may be, they are a race penned apart to tell you the truth. That is why I shouldn't mind consulting a priest forty times a day on any point where I thought he would help me to see the truth, but that is not because you want to shelve the responsibility, it is because you are taking the responsibility, ... and you want to be quite certain you are doing so.

But I quite admit there may be millions of stupid Catholics or wicked Catholics or any kind, it doesn't affect to me the truth or the untruth of the thing ...

Yrs, M.B.

DAME ETHEL SMYTH   Pickwick's Villa, Dulwich Village,
London, S.E. 21
Sunday, October 25 [?], 1919

Beloved E.,

... On rereading your letter I thought at first I had been guilty of bad theology and loose writing in comparing the priest to *Bradshaw* but on thinking it over I am not sure. *Bradshaw* doesn't tell you where to go, he only tells you where the trains go and what time they start. The priest's business is to tell you the truth about the journey and to tell you plainly that the South Western won't take you to Scotland.

The authority for the journey is the word of God. The choice the will of man. I think it is bad theology to say that the priest directs your trains. But no non-Catholic will believe this. (As you know, the whole of Catholic theology and philosophy is founded on that belief in <u>free-will</u> and this to me was a great difficulty.)

No doubt hundreds of people misuse priests ... but theologically the priest is only an instrument and when you confess to a priest you confess to <u>God</u> and not to the priest. All, or nearly all, non-Catholics think, and I certainly used to think, that the fact of confession must lead to a shelving of responsibility and to generally making things slacker. But it is not so in practice (according to my experience).

[133]

In practice confession is like taking a <u>tonic</u>; you feel very well after it but every time it is disagreeable in the taking and it is a perpetual reminder of your own responsibility. You are perpetually reminded of your journey. But I won't bore you any more.

What led me from the philosophy of 'religion and no <u>creed</u>' was a line of Goethe's, '*Nur das Gesetz kann uns die Freiheit gaben*'.[1] I realized that this was true first in art then in politics (Russia, etc.) and then I came to think it must be true as regards religion. And in Anglicanism there seemed to be no 'Gesetz' or a 'Gesetz' made elastic and out of all recognition. And that is what I think now, that in becoming a Catholic you bow your head under a narrow door to enter infinite space and infinite freedom. ...

Yrs, M.B.

1 'Only through the law can we attain freedom.'

EDMUND GOSSE   Tregenna Castle Hotel, St Ives, Cornwall
April 18th, 1894. no. 1920

Beloved Chermaître,

Here I sit in the same hotel and I fancy in the same sitting room whence Henry James wrote to you in August 1894. Jack Squire is here but alas! goes away tomorrow. I shall miss him dreadfully. He has looked after me like an angel. (I have been ill during the last five weeks but I am getting well rapidly.) While I was laid up at Dulwich I asked Evan [Charteris] to bring you down to see me but he couldn't manage it. We (Jack and I) have been reading Henry James's letters. We can't both help wishing you had edited them. Lubbock is a little too reverent.[1] 'Don't read *The Times* with such a reverent face,' as my Aunt said, when she was dying, to her daughter Betty.

But we have enjoyed the letters: they are a fine and impressive record of a great intellect and of its inner workings. As letters (and judged solely as such) I do think they lack intimacy and familiarity, but as a projection of the great artist's mind they are unique. As a letter writer I prefer Horace Walpole and Lamb and Byron and yourself. He lends colour to Wilde's aphorism that a great artist cannot admire any other great artist. Not from jealousy or rivalry but from impossibility, to which H. J. owns a thousand times – not wanting to reconstruct the work in question in

[134]

his own fashion. He admits no form but his own. Not Flaubert's, nor Hardy's nor Meredith's nor Tolstoi's. And Tolstoi has form sometimes, I should say always, but a form of his own and most unlike H. J.'s.

… We have been to the Lizard but not to Penzance because of the Pirates who are said to be very active this year. We have also been to a place with a name like Zoedont where we had a rich tea, saffron cake and clotted cream.

I can only walk a little but I drive with the air of a dowager. I am going to stay here probably another fortnight. …

Love to all,

Yrs M.B.

1 Percy Lubbock (1879–1965) had edited a selection of Henry James's letters, just published.
For the reply to this letter see Charteris pp. 462–3.

EDMUND GOSSE   Tregenna Hotel, St. Ives, Cornwall
                                                                  April 23, 1920

Beloved Chermaître,

It was indeed a treat to get your letter this morning. I lay in bed and revelled in it. You must at once let me know when the presentation is to take place on the 10th – auspicious day – so that I may be there in spirit if not in the body but I hope to be there in the body.[1] I am rapidly getting well, although yesterday – tell Jack Squire if you see him – *j'ai commis une imprudence*. Namely I worked too hard with Hugh Cecil in trying to divert a stream – the current of the stream – on the beach of Carbis Bay. The children of the place looked on in amazement at the spectacle of an elderly politician and a bald grey-haired swathed invalid on their hands and knees in the sand and the sewage pulling up rocks, hurling stones, their faces and sleeves covered with wet sand, sweating, straining, groaning, panting, striving, moaning but never giving in, till the rocks were lifted and the rebellious, reluctant stream was forced to obey their will![2] What would our Nannies say, the children seemed to think. The result was I was overtired, and paid for it, but I am well today and ready to begin again. We visited the Lizard the other day but we didn't see its tail. …

I have finished Henry James's letters with a gasp of admiration. I should have liked more letters as I feel there must be many more. Huge chunks of his life are jumped over with the agility of a goat. One rises from this perusal in deep obeisance before so great an intellect and wholehearted gratitude to an all-seeing and ingenious Providence in having created so unique a being and in having given us the joy of seeing English life through his temperament and seeing it contrasted with American life. Also at having there recorded the complete artist.

During the last three years I have read all Henry James's works. I read as far as *The Golden Bowl* during the war and half through [it] I stuck and read not one word more, but when Peace was declared and the trees opened their young adventurous arms to greet the Spring ... I took it up again and read it all, and quite see that read quietly in peace time there is not a word, not a comma, to omit, not to mention that it contains some of the most subtle and powerful scenes he ever conceived. But I sometimes wonder whether all that elaboration of H.J.'s third manner is worth while, whether the subject and the substance are worth the elaboration of treatment? And whether after all his most successful frame *toile* work was not the *nouvelle*, a framework the size of *The Spoils of Poynton*.

But that is no doubt a heretical doubt. And I am glad we possess all three of his manners. As for complete sympathy I divide all artists as far as my personal sympathies are concerned into two classes, those who like poetry and those who don't. When they don't, I never have complete sympathy with them. I feel H.J. didn't. While Jack [Squire] and I were discussing H.J the other day, Hugh Cecil, who was reading a quoted passage of the Master, said he had a bad ear and he quoted a fine passage ending with the word 'flap', which he said a man with a good ear would never have done. This had never struck me before. Before we had begun to read the book, I said to Jack, talking of the French, that I thought they were totally uninterested in any art or literature outside their own country and they lived within a Chinese wall and lo! H.J. makes exactly the same remark after his first *séjour* in Paris.

How wise he was to come to London. One of his books I admire enormously is *The Bostonians* which he omitted from the collected, revised (and to my mind mutilated) edition, but which he talks of with toleration in the letters ...

Yrs, M.B.

1 Gosse was given a bronze bust of himself by Sir William Goscombe John. More

than 200 of his friends subscribed, including M.B. The presentation was made by
A. J. Balfour. A caricature by Max Beerbohm of Gosse's friends, including M.B.,
at the presentation of the bust is reproduced in Charteris at p. 444.
2 Lord Hugh Cecil (1869–1956) was staying at the same hotel. Son of 3rd
Marquess of Salisbury, Conservative M. P. 1895–1906 and 1910–37. Had served
in the R.F.C. P.C. 1918. Provost of Eton 1936–44. Cr. Baron Quickswood 1941.

DAME ETHEL SMYTH   Beaufort Castle, Beauly, N.B.
                                                September 2, 1922

Beloved E.,

... I have been reading [your] *Impressions that Remained*.¹ One of
the greatest, the supreme pleasures in life is, I think, to take up a book
saying to oneself, 'It is no use my reading that now as I know and
remember it too well', and then beginning it to find you have forgotten
so much of it that the second or third reading is better than the first. I
think I had already read it three times. This is the fourth time I have
read it, and I seem to see and hear all sorts of things that had escaped
me, and the whole of it is to me absolutely new and fresh. It made me
realize the reason of the point you mention, why I left out my mother.²
As I read the description you give of your mother I realized that I could
not write down and make such a portrait ...

My father was just as near but I was older when he died and you
were older when your mother died. You knew your mother as a grown
up person and I never knew my mother except as a schoolboy. And yet
that is not the reason, not the complete reason. The reason is not, I
think, that she was too near me but that I am too like her. I don't know
if this is true ... I do not see her as a person apart. I could tell stories
about her but ... I don't see her from the outside at all. ...

Even if I could have done it, I don't know that I would. This is
another question. And the reason of this is that my love for her was so
great, so immense, so wholehearted and fundamental, and the shock of
her death such an earthquake, that I couldn't stir up those embers and
make something out of it for the public eye.

But that wouldn't prevent me writing something for you. And I realize I couldn't even do that and so I think the reason must be that we
were too close together; there was too much of the same paste in our
compositions ...

[137]

Mrs Cornish died at the beginning of August. She had a short illness (heart) and it only lasted about a fortnight. During the first week of it she continued to be passionately interested in life and reread *Middlemarch* and then when she realized that she was dying she became still more passionately absorbed in what is beyond life, so that it was the happy end of a very full and breathlessly occupied life, a happy life shot with Sorrow and Tragedies but rich in 'vast consolations'. 'I have poured into them vast consolations', Thomas à Kempis. ...

Bless you, M. B.

1 An autobiography, 1919.
2 M.B.'s autobiography *The Puppet Show of Memory* was published in 1922.

TO AN ANONYMOUS REVIEWER
[IN FACT NAOMI ROYDE-SMITH]   3, Gray's Inn Square, W.C.1
July 10, 1925

Dear Sir,

I happened to be in my publisher's office yesterday and, while I was waiting, I looked at an enormous book which is kept there like the book of the Recording Angel, of all the reviews of the books published by him; and as I was looking through this I came upon a review about my book *Half a Minute's Silence* which came out in the *Daily News* and which I had not seen.

It gave me great pleasure and although I know it is wrong ever to answer a review, I can't help wishing to talk to you about one or two points you mention.

The first story wasn't suggested by *The Cherry Orchard*, although I saw that play acted in Moscow during the first week of its production in 1904, but by a country house visit I paid in the South of Russia later in 1907, where there was just such a large gathering of people as I describe, and the hostess told me later she <u>had</u> been thinking of the tree during the silence: the actual story was suggested and written the afternoon of the first Armistice day on which for the first time the two minutes silence was observed.

It may amuse you to know that I was the first person to mention Chekhov as a playwright in the English press. I saw his *Uncle Vania* acted in 1904 at Moscow and wrote an account of it and sent it to the

Saturday Review, but it was refused as they said the play was uninteresting and incoherent. I published the article, though, in the *Morning Post* as a piece of war correspondence on the way to Manchuria!

About the Shakespeare story, Shakespeare wasn't meant to be a ghost story and it wasn't meant to be in any [way] a creepy story. I wanted the reader to postulate the appearance of Shakespeare in the flesh, to think that is how he would have behaved if he had been there. You may say this is an impossible postulate. So it is. But the story was meant to be wholly satiric and had I meant it to be half a ghost story I should have tried to treat it differently.

I was much pleased, flattered indeed, by all the kind things you said.

Yours very truly,
Maurice Baring

DAME ETHEL SMYTH   White's
July 29, 1925

... If one has anything to do with play-writing, play-acting, play-producing – public performance – one must make up one's mind either to bully or be bullied. Sardou, Dumas, Gilbert, Shaw, Pinero bullied. Tchekov was bullied and I think died of it. The Goncourts were bullied and, oddly enough, I believe, D'Annunzio. Shakespeare, Molière – who knows?

What I have found in my life hardest to bear is the patronage from theatrical managers, agents, critics: 'One day, you'll write a play.' 'I should like, when you write a play...!' 'Of course, you understand it's not a play.'

Some weeks ago I went to a prize fight at the Albert Hall. How refreshing to see the British public face to face with <u>an</u> <u>art</u> (an art, mind you, and possibly genius) that they <u>liked</u> <u>and</u> <u>understood</u>. There was the same warm, tense, embracing silence, the same sudden tremor and irrepressible ripple of appreciation, the same unchokeable outburst of applause, face to face with a clever piece of footwork, an inspired punch, a subtle feint, a faultless piece of timing, as you find in a French theatre when [an] actor of genius is speaking Racine, or in a German concert hall where a violinist in a quartet is phrasing as if the composer were whispering in his ear.

M.B.

Come in a rag or in a skin,
In feathers or in brindled hair;
Come clothed in light or masked in sin,
Come anyhow from anywhere;
Come penniless or soaked in rum,
Come, walking on your hands, but come.

Come twiddling in fantastic reels,
Come in a kilt or in a skirt
Come with your breeches at your heels
& never mind about your shirt;
Come at a profit or a loss,
But come, appear, be present, Gosse!

[There followed a sketch map showing the way to M.B.'s flat in Gray's
Inn.]

DAME ETHEL SMYTH   3, Gray's Inn Square, W.C.1
                                             28, no 29 August, 1925

Dst. E.,
    … *Cruise of the Nona*[1]….what a delightful kind of book. I mean the
kind when a man's real daily table talk gets over the footlights of print.
So rare…

I know people who have sailed with Belloc. I have only been in a
motor boat with him…and those things do happen, they say; it is terribly dangerous, and I wouldn't go for a sailing expedition alone with
B[elloc] without a professional sailor for the world. He very nearly
drowned Freyberg, the V.C., a man who swum the Channel the other
day.[2] All the sails got into a tangle, and Freyberg had to jump into the
sea and with a rope in his teeth bring the *Nona*, or perhaps it was a
smaller craft, back to the harbour.

But the great gift B. seems to me to have pre-eminently is vision; and
as someone said to me who knows him better than anyone – someone
who was at school with him… says he was just the same then; 'his gift
of vision is such that he will enlighten you even in the provinces and
about the matters he is most ignorant of, and most wrong about as a

rule. For instance he knows nothing, or little, of Germany and about the Germans really; but even about the Germans he had made me, who knows the Germans well, and who have lived in Germany for years, see things I had never seen before' – but the point I, M.B., have noticed is this: at first sight he seems to you entirely wrong-headed, at second sight and after due reflection you think he is impossibly wrong-headed with patches and flashes of sense, and what a pity ... then after years, ten years, fifteen years, it suddenly dawns on you sometime, not that he has always been right about the very points ... where you thought him most wrong and most wrong-headed. Points now admitted by universal consent.

This is not only my experience but also that of people who hardly know him (Hugh Cecil for instance). And in my life I have seen some of the things which he said, and which when he said them were scouted as being the last word of absurdity, become commonplace in the leaders of the *Morning Post*. ...

Yrs, M.B.

1 By Hilaire Belloc, just published.
2 Bernard Freyberg (1889–1963) a New Zealander who won the V.C. in 1916 and the D.S.O. with 3 bars in the two world wars. G.C.M.G. 1946, etc. He was governor-general of New Zealand 1946–52 and cr. Baron in 1951. One of M.B.'s friends.

ARNOLD BENNETT   3 Gray's Inn Square, London, W.C.1
                              27th January 1926

Yes. But I think there is a lot more to be said. Of course if you say [Henry James] doesn't hold your attention then all is up, but I should like to hear a few things.

Do the novels and stories of his first manner not hold your attention?

The Portrait of a Lady, The Bostonians, The Tragic Muse, Daisy Miller, A London Life, surely the characters here are clear cut and alive? Do the novels of his second manner fail to hold – *The Spoils of Poynton, The Coxon Fund, The Aspern Papers, Glasses, The Altar of the Dead,* these *nouvelles*? As to the third manner, I stuck in *The Golden Bowl* twice, three times, [the] third time I read it, and I have read it twice, some of it three or four times, and I do think it a wonderful achievement, very largely due to the intolerably dictated parenthetical style; but what wonderful scenes, what tense drama of the Soul at times – the scene on the staircase between Mr and Mrs Assingham, the Bridge Scene – and the whole story is to me poignant, subtle and true. I think *The Wings of a Dove* better still because there he creates a special character, the crystal-clear American girl which he has done so well. I think his real trouble is that his style, distinguished and accurate and cultured as it is, is not mature English, it has no savour. It grows from no soil, it is an exotic and vitiated by dictation, by the 'terrified desire to say everything' (quotation from parody of Henry James by Maurice B.).

In spite of all this I think he is a great artist and a great novelist, unique in some ways. I have read all his novels many times and all his stories. I can't read his memoirs [any] more than you can. I think to say he doesn't understand public houses is like accusing Watteau and Boucher of not being Hogarth, but I should never have read his later books had there not been a European War. I should never have read *The Golden Bowl* had I not had a serious illness.

Yrs, Maurice

P.S. It is very important what mood you are in when you approach H. J. In some moods he is intolerable just as in some moods you would not want to hear Debussy.

VERNON LEE

Royal York Hotel, Brighton,
where I am recovering from influenza.
I go back to London tomorrow –
3 Gray's Inn Square, London, W.C.1
April 5, 1926

'They have nothing to do except to go to parties.' Words taken from a letter of Vernon Lee's to M. B. ...

Here are a few points for your consideration ...

1 [On] *les classes aisées* (to which you and I belong, dear Vernon, let us never forget that) ... There is only one difference, one gulf in material conditions that really vitally matters and that is not – as the muddle-headed so often say – the gulf between he who has £800 a

year and £5,000,000,000 but the gulf between precarious living, the possible daily nothing, and something. Between your manner of life and a Rothschild there is only a small difference of degree; but between my charwoman's manner of life and yours and mine there is an infinite gulf because hers is precarious. Well, is it not possible, I say, that *les classes aisées* are not more innocently employed going to parties than working on Committees, 'preventing the poor', doing things with charity associations that have terrible results? …

2 It is surprising how much time is taken up by parties in the lives of busy men. Henry James puts on record 244 dinner parties in one year! Robert Browning between 1870 and 1880 would have beaten that I think. Arthur Balfour, now nearly 80, would NOW beat them all. You yourself have been to many parties in Rome, London, Paris, etc.

3 Nothing seems to stop parties, neither death, earthquake, war, air-raids nor revolutions nor plague. Cf. Decameron, London Plague, French Revolution, Russian Revolution, the War.

Explanation? The unconquerable gregariousness of man?

4 When the reviewers of High (and Low) Brow newspapers say – as they did and do – about my puppets, 'they do nothing but go to parties', their indignation is, I think, not against the X party but the X2 of [a] party in Mayfair and Belgravia.

They have nothing to say against people who go to parties in Bloomsbury or Chelsea but when they profess to be shocked by the kind of parties I remember in my childhood – of which what is described in *Cat's Cradle* is a pale reflex – parties at my father's or Mrs P. Wyndham's or Leighton's, where a small group of (at least) decently clothed and (at least) civilly mannered people listened to music made by Beethoven, Mozart, Schubert and Rossini and played by Joachim, Madame Schumann, Madame Néruda, Ries, Piatti, or sung by Santley and Trebelli, and when I compare this to parties I have seen given by the modern 'intelligentsia' in Bloomsbury and Chelsea where … well the tone is different and sometimes (to the unmarried) *à faire rougir des singes*, I find them comic. And here, Vernon Lee, you writer of Essays, is a subject made to your hand.

Yrs, M.

[143]

Rhymes for the Times
A Ballade of the Beerless

The Colonies are going dry,
  The States from Oregon to Maine;
And even in the Isle of Skye
  You have to drink the falling rain.
I am as thirsty as a Dane;
I hope I made the matter clear;
I'm ready for the dead of Cain;
  I want a glass of decent beer.

The fitters in the workshop cry,
  The sailor in the 'Mary Jane',
The farmer in his field of rye,
  The smith, the soldier and the swain;
The waggoner upon his wain;
  The tinker, tailor, cobbler, seer
Are crying out but all in vain;
  'I want a glass of decent beer.'

I want to know the reason why
  Our ancient liberties are slain;
What secret, mute conspiracy
  Compels a nation to abstain;
I'd like to understand the gain
  If dope is substitute for cheer,
And want of malt suggests cocaine;
  I want a glass of decent beer.

Envoi

Prince, you have magnums of champagne,
  Fermented in the golden year,
Madeira, sherry straight from Spain.
  I want a glass of decent beer.

[Sent with a short covering letter.]

ANDRÉ MAUROIS   3, Gray's Inn Square, W.C.1
                                                    May 16, 1927

... Maintenant Diszy. C'est admirable, admirable, admirable.[1]...
Vous nous avait donné un Diszy vraiment vivant, aussi vivant que les
personages de ses livres (et je viens de relire *Endymion* qui est selon moi
un document très précieux). Il n'y a pas trop de politique et il y en a
assez. Les proportions du livre sont admirables et puis c'est senti, c'est
dramatique et c'est joli. Merci de ce rare plaisir. Vous avez rendu lisible
l'illisible ... et la tâche était pourtant rude quand on a non seulement la
tradition mais les propres écrits, les discours et les romans de Diszy lui-
même.

Félicitations.

Critiques. Vous en voulez? Une seule.

Il me semble en amoindrisant Gladstone vous amoindrissez Diszy.
Vous ne lui donnez pas un adversaire digne de lui... Sauf jusqu'à la fin
lorsque vous arrivez au Midlothian campaign, vous n'avez pas donné
au lecteur un seul soupçon que Gladstone était autre choise qu'un puri-
taine insupportablement ennuyeux. Vous n'avez jamais parlé de son
génie et son génie était le génie de l'orateur. Vous parlez de Beaconsfield
ayant du génie comme orateur. On a l'impression que Gladstone
répondait lourdement ... un pédant, un écossais. Mais non. Gladstone
comme orateur était un des plus grands qui ont jamais existé. Je l'ai
entendu parler trois fois, deux fois à la chambre, une fois pendant une
heure. C'etait Jaurès; c'était Briand; c'était encore davantage; c'était
comme le jeu d'un très grand acteur. ...

Vous avez fait un très beau livre. Il y a de bons livres et il y a qui sont
en même temps délicieux. C'est rare.

                                                            M.B.

[1] André Maurois had just published his *La Vie de Disraëli*, translated into
English as *Disraeli* the same year.

ARNOLD BENNETT   3, Gray's Inn Square, London, W.C.1
                                                    August 3rd, 1928

Dear Arnold,

I have been enjoying your articles in the *Evening Standard*. The one
about Edgar Wallace and the last one.[1] I think I have read over forty

books by Edgar Wallace and I now feel I am surfeited and that I shall never read another but I dare say I shall.

I thought what you said about the French language profoundly true – I would say it was the most difficult of all languages. ... If one knows a little French, as I do, one is at once aware of how little one knows, that one knows nothing. Russian, which is a simpler language in construction than either French or German, is nevertheless so difficult to manipulate instinctively that nobody, even a Russian, can do so without mistakes unless he has learned it as a child. It is like playing the piano, like reading at sight. You are aware of your mistakes too late.

Talking of coffee I met a coffee expert the other day, a Portuguese. We asked him why all coffee in English houses was nasty. He said 'May I look at your beans?' The beans were sent for. He looked at them and said 'These beans are excellent but every one of them has a flaw in it from the roasting. One badly roasted bean will spoil the coffee.' French farmers' wives I have seen myself spend a three quarters of an hour roasting and then remove the beans at the critical moment; a second too long and the coffee is ruined. Who is going to take the trouble to do that in England?

I am glad you said a word for Zola, although what you said would probably be unintelligible to any Frenchman who is less than forty – but that proves nothing except the march of the wheel of fame.

Maurois, when he was here the other day and lunched with me, was surprised that all my guests had read practically all Zola. I think the most perfect thing he ever wrote was *L'Attaque au Moulin*. I should choose as his four best novels *Terminal*, then *L'Assommoir*, *La Débâcle*, and *Au Bonheur des Dames*. I think *Nana* falls off in the second half except for the very end. His early novels interest me too in another way and *Un Page d'Amour* has some magnificent pictures; so does *La Faute de l'Abbé Mouret*.

I don't think Andrew Lang's work is all dead.[2] If you collect his first editions, which I did when I collected until four years ago, the prices are very high and many of his books still sell. ... I think he has written a great deal of beautiful and easy prose and some of the best criticism, witness *Letters to Dead Authors*, *Letters on Literature*, *Essays in Little*, *Lost Leaders*, and the translation of Theocritus [is] a masterpiece. If all good writing is to perish just because the name no longer commands respect to a reviewer then there is an end of all good writing. ...

Yrs., M.B.

1 At this time A.B. was writing what he described as 'easily the highest paid book articles in the world' for the *Evening Standard*. That on Edgar Wallace appeared on 19 July and that on the French books on 2 August. Wallace (1875–1932) was a journalist and author best remembered for his detective stories. He wrote about 170 books. At the time of this letter his play *The Squeaker* was running at the Apollo.
2 (1844–1912), Scottish scholar and author.

VIRGINIA WOOLF   Half Way House, Steyning Road, Rottingdean
September 23, 1933

Dear Virginia,

I have just finished *Buck's Book* and enjoyed it immensely.[1] He told me – I saw him 2 days ago – that when the book was finished his publisher read it and cut out half of it and then the publisher's solicitor read it and cut out another quarter for fear of libel, but by that time the book was printed in page; so the publisher wrote to him and said we have so many blank pages please send the requisite number of stories. This was done to me over my first book in 1904. Please add, said Methuen, 10,000 words before next Monday, and I answered as wiser men have answered after me, 'Yes, if you don't mind what words and in what order.'

To go back to Buck's book, what struck me was that every now and then he does get his own particular humour across the book – footlights which 'humorists' in other lines never do – cf. George Robey[2] (latest example). I remember Vernon Lee reading Kropotkin's *Memoirs* and saying 'That is the raw stuff of which *War and Peace* is the reflection.' I feel Buck's book is the raw stuff of which P.G. Wodehouse is the reflection. I told him you had read his book; he was delighted. He is a great personality.

Yours, Maurice

1 By Herbert Buckmaster, founder of Buck's Club. It includes a speech made by M.B. at a dinner in the club.
2 Born George Edward Wade (1869–1954), comedian. C.B.E. 1919, Kt. 1954. He had just published a volume of autobiography, *Looking Back on Life*.

18 Cheyne Row, Chelsea, S.W.3
                                             January 4, 1934

My dearest Hilary,

Your letter moved me to tears. I don't deserve such words but none the less they are like balm. There is nothing really serious the matter with me, as far as I know, only *des indices*, the creakings that happen in a door in time but forewarn the end which may be long distant. Distant or near, be assured of one thing. I realize and give thanks for the privilege of having known you, and be sure of this, but for you I should never have come into the Church: you were the lighthouse that showed me the way, the beacon, and once I was there you remained a tower of strength in times or moments of difficulty and we both agree that that is the only thing that matters. ...

God bless you,

Your thankful
Maurice

EDWARD MARSH   Half-Way House, Steyning Road, Rottingdean
                                             September 22nd, 1937

My dear Eddie,

... You can have lunch here if you like, but I have all my meals by myself as I can only sit at a table for five minutes.

Ethel's news is based entirely on her own buoyant optimism. My general health is perfect, but I cannot walk a yard; I cannot sit on a chair for more than ten minutes, and when I lie down I have fits of shaking all day long, and these wake me four or five times in the night. It is like having an angry wasp inside one's chest. I cannot hold a book in my hands and I can only bear being read to at times. Last night I had to call for the nurse three times and I often have to change my bed. Ethel has told all my friends I am much better, even those in Germany. The result is she has greatly added to the burden of my correspondence.

Yours, M.B.

P.S. It tires me very much to dictate. I had a violent attack in the middle of this letter and had to have a brandy and go to bed, where I am now finishing it.

Appendix

When Maurice Baring died Lord Trenchard sent the following appreciation to *The Times*.

> Major Maurice Baring was on the staff of Headquarters R.F.C. He had met me when I first landed in France. I had always intended to sack him as I did not know him and I could not think he was doing any good, but the very first day he showed me his complete lack of self-interest, his complete honesty, and his wonderful loyalty to Sir David Henderson and others. He was a genius at knowing the young pilots and airmen. He knew more about what mattered in war and how to deal with human nature, how to stir up those who wanted stirring up, how to dam down those who were too excitable, how to encourage those who were new to it, and in telling me when I was unfair more than any other man I know. He was a man I could always trust. He was my mentor and guide, and if I may say so, almost my second sight in all the difficult tasks that came in future years. In the words of a great Frenchman, 'there never was a staff officer in any country, in any nation, in any century like Major Maurice Baring'. He was the most unselfish man I have ever met or am likely to meet. The Flying Corps owed to this man much more than they know or think. His *R.F.C. H.Q.* should be read and re-read even partially to understand this great man. He never once failed me and only once lost his temper with me, though I must have tried him highly. All the juniors had confidence in him. It was he who brought the tone of 'service' into the R.F.C. and brought into it altogether a feeling of doing service to help other men and save lives in the Army on the land and in the Navy at sea. I can pay him no higher tribute; words fail me in describing this man.

Select Bibliography

Letley, Emma, *Maurice Baring, A Citizen of Europe*, 1991
Lovat, Laura, *Maurice Baring, A Postscript*, 1948 (contains letters)
Smyth, Dame Ethel, *Maurice Baring*, 1938 (contains letters)

The following list is by no means exhaustive as Maurice Baring was mentioned in many biographies and autobiographies of his period.

Abdy, Jane, and Gere, Charlotte, *The Souls*, 1984
Barker, Dudley, *G. K. Chesterton*, 1973
Bibesco, Princesse Marthe, *Le Confesseur et les Poètes*, 1970 (contains letters)
Boyle, Andrew, *Trenchard*, 1962 (contains photographs)
Buckmaster, Herbert, *Buck's Book*, 1933
Chaigne, Louis, *Maurice Baring*, 1935
Charteris, Evan, *The Life and Letters of Sir Edmund Gosse*, 1931 (contains many letters to M.B.)
Chaundy, Leslie, *A Bibliography ... of the Works of Maurice Baring*, 1925
Chesterton, G. K., *Autobiography*, 1937
Connolly, Cyril, *A Romantic Friendship: The Letters of Cyril Connolly to Noel Blakiston*, ed. Noel Blakiston, 1975
Connolly, Cyril, *Journal and Memoir*, ed. David Pryce-Jones, 1983
Cooper, Diana, *The Rainbow Comes and Goes*, 1959
Cooper, Diana, *The Light of Common Day*, 1959 (contains photograph)
Cooper, Diana, *Trumpets from the Steep*, 1960
Cooper, Duff, *Old Men Forget*, 1954 (contains extract from letter)
Douglas, Sholto, *Years of Combat*, 1963
Fleury, Serge, *Du Haut de Ma Falaise*, 1963
Gunn, Peter, *Vernon Lee*, 1964
Hassall, Christopher, *Edward Marsh*, 1959

Haynes, E. S. P., *Fritto Misto*, 1924

Horgan, Paul, *Maurice Baring Restored*, 1970

Jebb, Louis, 'Hilaire Belloc and Maurice Baring: A Meeting of Minds', *Chesterton Review*, 1988, vol. XIX, no. 1, and other articles in the same issue

Kernahan, Coulson, *Six Famous Living Poets*, 1922

Las Vergnas, Raymond, *Chesterton, Belloc, Baring*, 1938

Lauroukine, Nina, 'Maurice Baring and D. S. Mirsky: A Literary Relationship', *Slavonic and East European Review* 62 (i), 1984

Leslie, Shane, *The Film of Memory*, 1938

Lucas, E.V., *Reading, Writing and Remembering*, 1932 (contains letters and a portrait)

Maclean, Veronica, *Past Forgetting*, 2002

Marsh, Edward, *A Number of People*, 1939 (contains letters)

Newsome, David, *On the Edge of Paradise*, 1980

Orpen, Sir William, *An Onlooker in France*, 1921

Pares, Bernard, *My Russian Memoirs*, 1931

Pares, Bernard, *A Wandering Student*, 1948

Pearce, Joseph, *Wisdom and Innocence: A Life of G. K. Chesterton*, 1996

Ponsonby, Magdalen (ed.), *Mary Ponsonby*, 1927 (contains a letter)

St John, Christopher, *Ethel Smyth, A Biography*, 1959 (contains letters)

Sheppard, Clare, *Lobster at Littlehampton*, 1995

Skinner, Cornelia Otis, *Madame Sarah*, 1967

Smith, G. S., *D. S. Mirsky, A Russian-English Life*, 2000

Smyth, Dame Ethel, *What Happened Next*, 1940 (contains letters)

Speaight, Robert, *The Life of Hilaire Belloc*, 1957

Speaight, Robert (ed.), *Letters from Hilaire Belloc*, 1958 (contains letters to Baring)

Storrs, Ronald, *Orientations*, 1939

Thwaite, Ann, *Edmund Gosse*, 1984

Ward, Maisie, *Gilbert Keith Chesterton*, 1945 (contains a letter)

Ward, Maisie, *Return to Chesterton*, 1952

Wilson, A. N., *Hilaire Belloc*, 1984

Wilson, Edmund, *The Devils and Canon Barham*, 1973

Woolf, Virginia, *A Reflection of the Other Person. The Letters of Virginia Woolf: Volume IV, 1929–1931*, ed. Nigel Nicolson, 1978

Woolf, Virginia, *The Sickle Side of the Moon. The Letters of Virginia Woolf: Volume V, 1932–1935*, ed. Nigel Nicolson, 1979

Woolf, Virginia, *Leave the Letters Till We're Dead. The Letters of Virginia Woolf: Volume VI, 1936–1941*, ed. Nigel Nicolson, 1980

Ziegler, Philip, *Diana Cooper*, 1981

Index